P9-CCO-567

WELCOME
WELCOME
WELCOME

Chocolate for Breakfast and Tea

B&B Innkeepers Share Their Finest Recipes

Photo notes

Page 1: Thorwood Inn, Hastings, MN
Page 3: Bill Paulson photo; styling by Bev Watkins; Mocha Chocolate Chip Scones from the Inn at Cedar Crossing, Sturgeon Bay, WI
Page 5: Jeff Frey photo
Page 6: Courtesy of Mary Zahn
Page 11: Bob Rashid photo; Black Forest Stuffed French Toast from Victorian Treasure B&B Inn, Lodi, WI
Page 12: Dan Reynolds photo
Page 16: Bob Rashid photo
Pasge 20: Tom Bagley photo
Page 21: Tom Bagley photo; styling by Gail Greco
Page 24: Dan Reynolds photo
Page 28: Dave Tate photo
Page 29: Tom Bagley photo; styling by Gail Greco
Page 35: Thomas A. Schneider photo; Toasted Walnut Fudge Bread, from The Willow Brook Inn B&B, Canton, MI
Pages 40 & 41: Thomas A. Schneider photos
Page 45: George W. Gardner photo
Page 49: Thomas A. Schneider photo
Page 51: Chocolate Lover's Muffins, from The Old Rittenhouse Inn, Bayfield, WI
Page 52: George W. Gardner photo
Pages 66 & 67: Bill Paulson photos; styling by Bev Watkins
Page 70: Louis A. Raynor photo
Pages 74 & 75: Bill Paulson photos; styling by Bev Watkins
Page 76: Scott Campbell photo
Page 77: Grant Huntington photo
Page 81: Chocolate Rum Pound Cake, from Angel Arbor B&B, Houston, TX
Pages 82 & 83: Bill Paulson photos; styling by Bev Watkins
Page 109: Tom Bagley photo; styling by Gail Greco

Published by **Down to Earth Publications**
1032 West Montana Avenue
St. Paul, MN 55117
800-585-6211

Library of Congress Cataloging-in-Publication Data
Zahn, Laura C., 1957–
Chocolate for Breakfast and Tea.
ISBN 0-939301-97-0
1. Breakfasts 2. Chocolate 3. Muffins, Breads and Coffeecakes 4. Desserts and Snacks 5. Bed and Breakfast Accommodations — U.S. — Directories
TX767.C5

Dewey System – Ideas and Recipes for Breakfast and Brunch - 641.52

Front cover photo of Chocolate Apricot Torte, courtesy of The Inn at Cedar Crossing, Sturgeon Bay, Wisconsin (recipe page 82)
Front cover inset photo courtesy of The Gosby House, Four Sisters Inns, Monterey, California (recipe page 102)
Back cover photo courtesy of Adams Edgeworth Inn, Monteagle, Tennessee (recipe page 12)
Many thanks to these inns and the others who shared their delicious recipes and wonderful stories!

Cover and text design by Kathryn Mallien, Camden, Maine
Printed in Hong Kong

Contents

Chocolate Notes
7

Entrees
11

Breads & Coffeecakes
35

Muffins, Scones & Popovers
51

Desserts for Breakfast, Tea-Time & Snacks
81

Recipe Index
120

Subject Index
121

List of Featured Inns by State
126

Elegant Victorian dining at the Old Rittenhouse Inn, Bayfield, Wisconsin

For Kathy,
my sister in chocolate

Chocolate Notes

Chocolate Confusion

Remember the days when you could ride your bike to the corner store and get a nickel candybar? It was probably a milk chocolate bar, or one covered in milk chocolate.

Never ones to avoid more of a good thing, we chocolate-lovers now have a dizzying array of chocolates available. Here's an attempt to sort out the baking-aisle confusion as it relates to these recipes.

About "White Chocolate"

Been wondering why there's no "white chocolate" in the grocery store baking section? You can buy "vanilla chips" or "white confection chips" or "premium white chips," but probably not "white chocolate chips."

It's because of the federal government. According to it, there's no such thing as white chocolate, in the U.S.A., anyway. The government won't let candymakers label this cocoa butter-based candy "chocolate" without it containing chocolate "liquor."

The other thing you need to know about the alleged "white chocolate" business is that there are several makers of white confection bars or chips or whatever they call it, and their products vary widely in their taste (unlike, say, real semisweet chips, which may vary in quality, but all pretty much taste like semisweet chocolate, as compared to milk chocolate, for instance). Some white stuff is merely sweet; some is sweet enough to make your eyebrows curl.

For that reason, and because many chocolate lovers really don't like white chocolate (why should they? It's not *real* chocolate! Just because they like chocolate doesn't mean they like jelly beans, does it?), most white chocolate recipes have been avoided in this book. It's used as a coating in a couple of the truffle recipes, but if you really despise the stuff, use cocoa powder or ground or grated chocolate

Low-Cholesterol Double Chocolate Muffins from Rancho San Gregorio, San Gregorio, California

for coating the truffles. (If you really like the stuff, you are not alone, but you will have to look elsewhere to satisfy your white confection sweet tooth.)

About Types of Chocolate and Cocoa

Stood in the grocery store lately and looked at the choices of chocolate chips, for instance? A regular grocery store will easily have five different brands (plus mini, regular and mega sizes) of semisweet chips alone (and we're not counting chocolate-*flavored* chips, because those should be outlawed, or mint chocolate chips or low-fat chocolate chips or candy-coated chocolate bits).

Because a new chocolate product seems to be developed daily, and because home cooks may not have access to fancy food suppliers that innkeepers/restauranteurs may, this book sticks pretty much to ingredients easily found in most grocery stores. (We aren't called "Down to Earth Publications" for nothing.)

▲ ***Cocoa.*** Of course, when we say "cocoa" in recipes, we mean "cocoa powder," not the liquid hot chocolate that is comforting on cold winter nights (and the rest of the day/year).

Regular-old cocoa is dark, bitter and unsweetened. "Dutch processed" has been alkalized and isn't so bitter. There are also sweetened and flavored cocoa powders available and cocoas by other names. Most of the time, these recipes call for the regular old bitter stuff.

As for baking/cooking chocolate, here is a list of the chocolates used in this book, printed in order of the least sweet first:

▲ ***Unsweetened*** is just what it says, pure chocolate liquor, without any additives for sweetening or flavoring (you don't want to eat this plain). To substitute for a 1-ounce square, use 3 tablespoons cocoa and 1 tablespoon shortening in the recipe.

▲ ***Bitter*** is sometimes also called "bittersweet" or "dark chocolate."

Chocolate Macadamia Muffins from Grandma's House B&B Inn, Orrville, Ohio

This is good for chocolate-dipped mints, for instance, when a sweet chocolate would be too much sweet. At this writing, bitter chocolate is found in bars only and not chips, so it must be melted, or grated or chopped in a food processor, best done when the chocolate is about 60 degrees. This is sweeter than unsweetened baking and cooking chocolate, and it is edible, even preferable, by those who love true dark chocolate. It may be more difficult to find in some grocery baking sections, however, than unsweetened or semisweet chocolate.

▲ ***Semisweet*** is still sweeter, but some people call this "bittersweet" or still consider it "dark chocolate," so it may be listed as this in the recipes. While it's not the same as "bittersweet" (above), frankly, your recipe from this book will probably be fine if you don't have bittersweet chocolate and use semisweet instead. (It may be fairly *different*, but perfectly acceptable.) To substitute for a 1-ounce square, use a 1-ounce square of unsweetened chocolate plus 1 tablespoon sugar. Semisweet is the traditional content of chocolate chips, and you can eat them plain just fine.

▲ ***Milk chocolate*** is the stuff of the traditional candy bar, and often too sweet for many baked goods that contain sugar, too.

The inviting parlor at Sea Crest by the Sea, Spring Lake, New Jersey

About Brands

Everyone's got their own preferences when it comes to chocolate, and this editor is not about to tell you which to buy. But expensive does not always mean best. On the other hand, least expensive usually means it's awful (chocolate-flavored chips, for instance, and not real chocolate). Some brands of chips melt better than others (chips are made to "stand up" to higher heat without melting so quickly, and some innkeepers complain about some brands being "too waxy," for instance). So shop around, experiment. Wouldn't it be terrible if you had to try every brand of semisweet chips at your local store?

Hint of Mint Chocolate Torte from the Inn at Olde New Berlin, New Berlin, Pennsylvania

About Melting Chocolate

Remember, this is Down to Earth Publications. We wish to bring you recipes you can actually make in a reasonable amount of time in a normal kitchen equipped with regular gadgets. Innkeepers, like most people in the real world, don't want to stay up 'til 2 A.M. to make a batch of truffles or whatever. That means many of them (the ones who don't employ professional chefs, for instance) are going to microwave their chocolate squares or chips to melt them.

The purists out there are now screaming or, at the least, their blood is racing. "Chocolate burns easily!" they are thinking. "You can't microwave it!"

Well, it *does* burn easily. And if you burn it, you will know. It will be a big seized-up mess (same thing happens if you get water in it) and you'll have to start over with new chocolate.

If you microwave it, that's the chance you take. But if you microwave it on a medium-high setting for 25 seconds, stir it, repeat, stir, repeat, etc., you're not going to burn it very often (for some of us, it only takes once to waste chocolate!). The time and mess you save by using one glass bowl in the microwave, rather than a double boiler, for instance, makes it worth the risk of burning. (If you don't agree, feel free to get out the double boiler.) Innkeepers have made these recipes over and over, and some of them melt their chocolate in a heavy saucepan over low heat on the stove (not recommended by Down to Earth unless you have a *really* heavy saucepan, commercial-kitchen quality).

Also, none of these recipes require the intimidating process of "tempering" chocolate, or anything else that's really difficult, for that matter. These recipes were tested in home kitchens and the innkeepers were asked to retest their recipe(s) as written in this book (most innkeepers are working in what would be considered home kitchens, afterall).

Inn-dulge in chocolate and inn-joy these fine inns—make a reservation sometime soon!

Entrees

Apricot Pancakes with Chocolate Orange Sauce

While Christopher Columbus was introduced to chocolate as a beverage in Nicaragua in 1502, it was Conquistador Hernán Cortés, given the bitter chocolate drink by Emperor Montezuma II and the Aztecs in 1519, who carried it back to share with Europeans.

These incredibly light, fluffy pancakes turn a gorgeous golden brown. The bits of dried apricot become chewy and warm and are delicious topped with the Chocolate Orange Sauce. (If you can't wait for the rich sauce, or want twice as much chocolate, add some mini semisweet chips to the pancake batter!)

⅔ to 1 cup snipped dried apricots
¾ cup boiling water
1¼ cups buttermilk
1 egg
3 tablespoons vegetable oil
1 cup flour
1½ tablespoons sugar
1½ teaspoons baking powder
1½ teaspoons baking soda
1 teaspoon salt, optional

Place the apricots in a heat-proof bowl and add boiling water to cover. When rehydrated, about 15 minutes, drain. Meanwhile, with an electric mixer, beat buttermilk, egg and oil.

In a separate bowl, mix flour, sugar, baking powder, baking soda and optional salt. Add flour mixture to buttermilk mixture and beat well. Then fold in drained apricots.

Ladle batter onto a hot, lightly oiled griddle. Cook over medium heat until puffed and dry around the edges (about 2 to 3 minutes; "scratch" pancakes take longer than the box ones). Flip and cook until golden brown on the other side, about 1 minute.

Remove pancakes, spread with melted butter and make stacks of 3, keeping warm until all pancakes are finished. Serve with Chocolate Orange Sauce.

Makes about 15 4-inch pancakes

Chocolate Orange Sauce

2 tablespoons butter
½ cup heavy cream
4 tablespoons corn syrup
4 ounces unsweetened chocolate
1 cup sugar
½ cup boiling water
2 teaspoons vanilla extract
½ teaspoon orange extract

In a heavy saucepan, place butter, cream, corn syrup, chocolate and sugar, stirring over low heat until chocolate and butter are melted and sugar is almost dissolved. Bring the mixture to a simmer, add the boiling water and stir to blend. Cook over medium-low heat for 5 minutes without stirring.

Remove the pan from the stove. Stir in the vanilla and orange extracts. Serve warm. (Refrigerate any leftovers for hot fudge sundaes.)

Makes about 2 cups

Adams Edgeworth Inn

This 1896 Queen Anne country house is set amid lushly landscaped grounds in Monteagle, Tennessee. Nested in a wilderness atop the Cumberland Mountains, this 96-acre private village of 150 Victorian cottages is easily toured on the inn's electric cart. Wendy and David Adams' National Register inn features Victorian decor, fine art, antiques, collector quilts and fine candlelight dining. The Adamses also restored and opened a beautiful stone mansion, Adams Hilborne Inn, in Chattanooga.

Adams Edgeworth Inn
Monteagle Assembly
Monteagle, TN 37356
615-924-4000
Fax 615-924-3236

Bittersweet Chocolate Souffles with White Chocolate and Rum Sauce

Fudgy yet light, these individual breakfast souffles become exotic treats with Chris Sprague's White Chocolate and Rum Sauce. These were a breakfast favorite at her Newcastle Inn in Newcastle, Maine, where she penned a popular cookbook, and they were an immediate hit at her new inn, The Inn at Ormsby Hill, Manchester Center, Vermont.

Butter and sugar to prepare ramekins
8 ounces bittersweet (or semi-sweet) chocolate, chopped
1 tablespoon unsalted butter
1 tablespoon flour
½ cup milk
3 egg yolks
1 teaspoon vanilla extract
4 egg whites
1 teaspoon lemon juice
¼ cup sugar
Powdered sugar

Lightly butter eight 6-ounce ramekins and dust them well with granulated sugar. Set them aside.

Melt the bittersweet chocolate in a double boiler, covered, over barely simmering water. Remove the cover and stir until the chocolate is smooth. Remove the top pan of the double boiler from the heat.

In a small saucepan, melt the butter over medium heat. Stir in the flour, and cook until the mixture is thick, but not browned, 1 to 2 minutes. Add the milk and whisk briskly until the mixture is smooth and thick, about 3 minutes.

Remove the pan from heat. Add the melted chocolate and whisk until smooth. Whisk in egg yolks and vanilla. Set pan aside.

With an electric mixer, beat the egg whites and lemon juice on medium speed until soft peaks form, about 1 minute. While beating at high speed, sprinkle the ¼ cup sugar on top and beat until the whites are stiff, but not dry. Using a rubber spatula, stir one-quarter of the whites into the chocolate mixture to lighten it, then fold in the remaining whites. Divide the mixture among the ramekins. At this point, the souffles can be refrigerated, uncovered, for up to 5 hours.

Preheat the oven to 375 degrees. Bake the souffles (on a cookie sheet, if you wish) for 17 minutes or until they are puffed and slightly cracked on top. Remove from oven, dust with powdered sugar and serve immediately with a pitcher of the White Chocolate and Rum Sauce.

Makes 8 souffles

White Chocolate and Rum Sauce

6 ounces finest white chocolate, chopped or grated
⅓ cup dark rum

In the top of a double boiler, slowly melt the white chocolate over simmering water. Whisk in the rum until it is completely incorporated. Remove the top of the double boiler from the heat, and let the sauce stand at room temperature. Serve in a pitcher at room temperature or slightly warm.

The Inn at Ormsby Hill

In 1995, Chris and Ted Sprague bought this 1764 home-turned-inn and began major renovation. Within nine months, nine of the 10 guestrooms had two-person whirlpool tubs and fireplaces. Chris and Ted aim to create a romantic retreat in this historic building. Its remarkable history includes serving as a hiding place for Ethan Allen, having the first electricity in a private home in Vermont, and being the site of the first jail cell in Manchester (yes, it's still in the cellar).

The Inn at Ormsby Hill
Manchester Center, VT
05255
802-362-1163

Black Forest Stuffed French Toast

No one leaves the table hungry after Kimberly Seidl's three-course breakfast. For many tastes, this recipe has just the right amount of chocolate for breakfast or brunch.

Black Forest Sauce:

1 16-ounce can pitted dark sweet cherries, in juice
¼ cup sugar
1 teaspoon vanilla extract
2 cups cold water
3 tablespoons cornstarch
¼ teaspoon grated nutmeg

French Toast:

2 8-ounce packages cream cheese, at room temperature
2 ounces semisweet chocolate, shaved or grated, or ½ cup miniature semisweet chocolate chips
5 eggs
1½ cups milk
1½ teaspoons sugar
1½ teaspoons vanilla extract
¼ teaspoon salt, optional
1 or 2 loaves French or Italian bread (about 5 inches wide and long enough for 12 thick slices)

Make Black Forest Sauce first: In a saucepan, heat cherries and juice. Stir in sugar and vanilla.

In a separate bowl, mix water and cornstarch. Stir into cherries, simmering until thickened, stirring frequently. Stir in nutmeg. Keep warm.

In a medium bowl, beat cream cheese until smooth. Stir in shaved chocolate or miniature chips. Set aside.

In a large bowl, beat eggs, milk, sugar, vanilla and optional salt.

Slice French bread into 12 slices, each 1 to 1½ inches thick. Then slice a pocket into the middle of each slice. Fill each pocket with ½ to 1 tablespoon cream cheese mixture.

Dip bread slices into egg batter on both sides. Place on a hot griddle and brown. Turn and brown on the other side. (Keep slices in a warm oven, if necessary, while finishing all 12 slices.)

To serve, place two slices on each plate and top with about ¾ cup warm Black Forest Sauce.

Makes 6 servings

Victorian Treasure B&B Inn

Located 20 minutes north of Madison in Wisconsin's beautiful River Country, the Victorian Treasure is an elegant retreat in a quiet and friendly small town. Kimberly and Todd Seidl welcome guests to their two historic Queen Anne Victorians. All the guestrooms have fine antiques and several feature whirlpools and fireplaces, too.

Victorian Treasure
B&B Inn
115 Prairie Street
Lodi, WI 53555
608-592-5199
800-859-5199

Chocolate Banana Crepes in Apricot Sauce

Innkeeper Lynn Savage's spectacular creation uses fresh Rogue River Valley apricots and contrasts a very sweet filling with an unsweetened chocolate crepe. It's versatile, too, and could be topped with whipped cream for a dessert crepe. (Note that where fresh, ripe apricots are not available, a 12-ounce bag of frozen peaches makes an acceptable substitute.) Or double the batch and fill extras with sweetened whipped cream or Bavarian Cream, page 20.

Crepe batter:
1 egg
1 tablespoon butter, melted
⅔ to ¾ cup milk
½ cup flour
¼ cup powdered Italian chocolate (or cocoa)
1 tablespoon sugar, optional

Apricot Sauce:
1 tablespoon butter
⅜ cup sugar
1½ tablespoons lemon juice
1 tablespoon cornstarch
Pinch of ground nutmeg
Pinch of cinnamon
3 cups fresh apricots, cut into sixths
⅜ cup water
2 tablespoons freshly squeezed orange juice
1 tablespoon fresh orange zest or peel

Banana Filling:
1 tablespoon butter
3 tablespoons brown sugar
1 tablespoon apricot marmalade or preserves
2 ripe-but-firm bananas
⅛ teaspoon cinnamon
⅛ teaspoon almond extract
⅛ teaspoon vanilla extract

Also:
Sour cream

For Crepes: Place egg, melted butter, ⅔ cup of the milk, flour, cocoa and optional sugar in a blender. Blend on high until smooth. If batter needs more milk, blend it in now.

Pour about ¼ cup batter per crepe onto a hot, non-stick pan or griddle. Swirl batter out to a thin pancake. Cook until the top dries to only a few beads of moisture (a few seconds), then flip and cook briefly on the other side. Set cooked crepes aside.

Makes 8 crepes

For Apricot Sauce: Melt butter over medium heat. Stir in sugar, lemon juice, cornstarch, nutmeg and cinnamon. Then mix in apricots and coat well. Cook, stirring occasionally, until the sauce thickens. Add water, orange juice and orange peel. Cook until sauce thickens again. Pureé the hot sauce in blender. Strain mixture, if you wish, and set aside.

For Banana Filling: Melt butter in a frying pan over low heat. Stir in brown sugar and marmalade, melting marmalade completely while stirring.

Cut bananas in half lengthwise, then slice in ¼-inch pieces. Cook bananas in sugar mixture on medium low heat for 2 to 4 minutes, turning gently until they are just soft. Add cinnamon and almond and vanilla extracts. Fold gently and remove from heat.

To Assemble: Preheat oven to 350 degrees. Spoon 6 slices of banana onto each crepe. Place 3 tablespoons or so of strained Apricot Sauce on the bottom of an ovenproof plate. Fold sides of crepe around the Banana Filling and place it, seam side down, on the sauce on the plate. Place two crepes on each plate. Top with about ¼ cup Apricot Sauce. Warm plates in the oven for 10 to 12 minutes. Serve with a dollop of sour cream.

Makes 4 servings

Hersey House

Innkeeper Lynn Savage and her sister, Gail Orell, bought this 1904 modified salt box home in 1983 and opened it as a B&B a year later. Guests dine on family china, overlooking the beautiful perennial and herb gardens the sisters have planted. The innkeepers are happy to help with arrangements to Ashland's famous Oregon Shakespeare Festival.

Hersey House
451 North Main Street
Ashland, OR 97520
541-482-4563
Fax 541-482-2839

Blue Harbor House,
Camden, Maine

Chocolate Brownie Souffle

The lightest brownies you'll ever eat. Hungry chocolate fanatics will eat two, so consider doubling the recipe. Whipped cream topping, with or without the rum, is a must!

Bavarian Cream:
2 cups milk
6 tablespoons sugar, divided
1 tablespoon vanilla extract
2 whole eggs
2 egg yolks
2 tablespoons cornstarch
2 tablespoons unsalted butter, cut into ½ teaspoon pieces

Brownie Souffles:
2 teaspoons unsalted butter, divided
2 tablespoons sugar, divided
1 ounce semisweet chocolate
½ cup Bavarian Cream
2 tablespoons cocoa
2 egg yolks
2 tablespoons chopped walnuts
3 egg whites
Heavy cream whipped with sugar and rum, to taste
Strawberries

Make the Bavarian Cream first: In a saucepan, scald mixture of milk, 3 tablespoons of the sugar and vanilla.

Meanwhile, in a medium bowl, beat remaining sugar, eggs, egg yolks and cornstarch. Slowly stir scalded milk into egg mixture. Return to saucepan. Cook custard slowly, stirring until desired thickness.

Remove from heat and return to mixing bowl. Stop further cooking by placing mixing bowl in a larger bowl with ice. Whisk until cool, adding butter a little at a time.

Store covered in the refrigerator. Can also be used for Neopolitans, or with bananas or coconut as pudding. Makes about 2½ cups.

Melt 1 teaspoon butter. Using a pastry brush, coat four 4- or 6-ounce ramekins with melted butter, then line with 1 tablespoon of the sugar. Refrigerate prepared ramekins until needed.

Preheat oven to 450 degrees.

In a double boiler or microwave, melt remaining 1 teaspoon butter and semisweet chocolate.

In the large bowl of an electric mixer, combine Bavarian Cream, cocoa, remaining 1 tablespoon sugar and melted chocolate. When mixture become smooth and creamy, mix in egg yolks, one at a time. (If mixture becomes too thick, add a small amount of milk until light and creamy.) Stir in walnuts.

In a separate bowl, whip egg whites until stiff. Fold egg whites into chocolate mixture. Then fill prepared ramekins three-quarters full.

Place ramekins on the wire oven rack and bake 8 to 12 minutes. When souffles are done they puff up and look like a small chocolate cake. While souffles are baking, whip cream and prepare strawberry garnishes. Remove from oven and serve immediately with whipped cream and garnish.

Makes 4 servings

Blue Harbor House

Innkeepers Jody Schmoll and Dennis Hayden, and their black lab, Bali, welcome guests to their inn in postcard-pretty Camden. The home of the first Camden settler, the inn is a restored 1810 New England Cape, complete with inn guestrooms and carriage house suites. Jody and Dennis serve exquisite candlelight dinners for guests, by reservation only, including a hearty Down East lobster feast.

Blue Harbor House
67 Elm Street
Camden, ME 04843
207-236-3196
800-248-3196

The Maples Inn

Innkeeper Susan Sinclair quit her job as vice president of a California bank and moved almost as far away as she could in the continental U.S. She entered the innkeeping profession in this lovely 1903 home on a quiet street in popular Bar Harbor. Her inn is a quick walk from Bar Harbor's restaurants and shops.

The Maples Inn
16 Roberts Avenue
Bar Harbor, ME 04609
207-288-3443

Chocolate Chip Pancakes

Before a day of hiking, biking or x-c skiing in Acadia National Park, whale watching, sailing or other outdoor activities along the Maine coast, guests at Susan Sinclair's Bar Harbor inn appreciate a hearty-yet-fun breakfast. Her Chocolate Chip Pancakes often take guests who've never tried them by surprise—they are scrumptious! And if there are children at the breakfast table, the whipped cream and extra chocolate chips become much-appreciated facial features on each pancake.

1¼ cups buttermilk
1 egg
2 tablespoons oil
1 cup flour
2 teaspoons baking powder
1 teaspoon sugar
½ teaspoon baking soda
½ teaspoon salt, optional
Up to 1 cup miniature semi-sweet chocolate chips
Whipped cream

In a small bowl, beat the buttermilk, egg and oil. Set aside.

In a large bowl, combine the flour, baking powder, sugar, baking soda and optional salt. Stir the buttermilk mixture into the flour mixture. Some lumps may remain.

Pour ¼ cup of batter for each 4-inch pancake onto a lightly greased griddle. Top each pancake with 12 to 15 miniature chips. Cook until edges become dry, then flip and cook briefly on the other side.

Keep pancakes warm until serving. Top with whipped cream and sprinkle with more chips, then serve with favorite syrups.

Makes 8 to 9 pancakes

Chocolate Fondue

"I like to serve this to honeymooners, sometimes as a leisurely breakfast in bed," says Innkeeper Leanne McClain. Most of her guests have never heard of it before—especially for breakfast! It is neither too sweet nor too heavy for morning fare and is absolutely delicious with fruit or pound cake, for instance. And if you heat the mixture in a heavy, heat-holding ceramic or glass bowl in the microwave, then eat soon thereafter, you don't even need a fondue pot!

1 12-ounce bag milk chocolate chips
¾ cup half 'n half
1 to 2 tablespoons kirsch, brandy, orange liqueur, coffee liqueur or instant coffee granules

Also:
Sliced bananas and/or apples
Fresh strawberries
Sliced fresh peaches, nectarines or plums
Grapes
Orange and/or grapefruit sections
Cubed banana bread, pound cake, or a similar sweet bread or muffins

In a large microwave-safe bowl, microwave the chocolate chips and half 'n half on medium-high for 25 second intervals, stirring in between, until melted and smooth. Stir in liqueur or coffee granules, stirring until dissolved. Pour into a fondue pot with a low flame underneath.

Arrange fruit and bread on a large platter, perhaps surrounding the fondue pot. Pierce the fruit or bread with a fondue fork, then dip in the warm chocolate mixture and immediately devour!

Makes 4 servings

Window on the Winds B&B

Leanne McClain is an archeologist who's turned her two-story log home at the base of the Wind River Mountains in western Wyoming into a comfortable four-guestroom B&B. Window on the Winds is located on the Continental Divide Snowmobile Trail at elevation 7,175 feet, within two hours of Jackson Hole. Guests return from fishing, rafting, riding, biking or skiing and enjoy the hot tub. Leanne specializes in Western hospitality, even offering to board guests' horses.

Window on the Winds
B&B
10151 Highway 191
P.O. Box 996
Pinedale, WY 82941
307-367-2600

Chocolate Chocolate Chip Waffles with Raspberry Syrup

Innkeeper and Executive Chef Wendy Adams' versatile waffles can be made with or without the chocolate chips. She loves including chocolate in her menus here and at the Adams Edgeworth Inn in Monteagle, Tennessee.

¾ cup sugar
½ cup butter, melted
2 eggs, separated
3 ounces bittersweet chocolate, melted and cooled
½ teaspoon vanilla extract
1½ cups flour
2 tablespoons baking powder
¼ teaspoon salt, optional
2 teaspoons instant coffee powder or granules
⅔ cup milk
½ cup semisweet chocolate chips or miniature chips

In the large bowl of an electric mixer, beat the sugar and butter. Then beat in egg yolks, chocolate and vanilla.

In a separate bowl, sift together the flour, baking powder, salt and coffee powder. Blend the flour mixture into the chocolate mixture by hand, alternating with the milk.

With an electric mixer, beat the egg whites until stiff but not dry. Fold them into the chocolate batter, then stir in the chocolate chips. The batter will be fairly thick, almost like brownie batter.

Ladle about ½ cup of batter onto a hot oiled waffle iron. Bake until crisp outside and dry inside, about 3 minutes per waffle.

Serve warm with Raspberry Syrup and topped with a dollop of Mocha Whipped Cream.

Makes 6 waffles

Raspberry Syrup

⅔ cup sugar
1 tablespoon cornstarch
Pinch of salt
1½ cups water
2 cups fresh raspberries

In a saucepan, mix sugar, cornstarch and salt until there are no lumps. Whisk in water and cook over medium-high heat until the mixture boils and thickens. Fold in raspberries and return the mixture to a boil.

Remove from heat. Strain to remove seeds and serve hot.

Mocha Whipped Cream

1 cup heavy cream
¼ cup strong, cold coffee
¼ teaspoon vanilla extract
⅓ cup superfine sugar (or granulated)

In the bowl of an electric mixer, combine cream, coffee and vanilla. Beat on high speed while slowly sprinkling in sugar. Beat until soft peaks form.

Adams Hilborne Inn

This impressive 1889 structure has become Chattanooga's premiere small European hotel, featuring 11 guestrooms, 16-foot coffered ceilings and Tiffany windows. Listed on the National Register of Historic Places and located in the Fortwood Historic District, the home originally was built for Mayor Edward G. Watkins. Wendy and David Adams undertook major restoration work and opened their highly acclaimed inn in 1995. Also featured is the Porch Cafe for bistro-style dining.

Adams Hilborne Inn
801 Vine Street
Chattanooga, TN 37403
423-265-5000
Fax 423-265-5555

Hersey House

Once the home to five generations of Herseys, this 1904 house has been lovingly restored by Lynn Savage and her sister, Gail Orell. They operate the popular B&B in a town famous for its Shakespearean summer stock. The Hersey House is famous for its use of regional foods in creative dishes, such as this one.

Hersey House
451 North Main Street
Ashland, OR 97520
541-482-4563
Fax 541-482-2839

Chocolate Raspberry Blintzes

"To live in Oregon is to enjoy berries in the summer and July is raspberry month," said Hersey House Innkeeper and Chef Lynn Savage. While she's served raspberry blintzes for years, she only recently created chocolate blintz batter as a natural partner for the local bounty. Consider doubling the batch of blintzes and freezing leftovers since the blintzes are also good at room temperature or slightly warmed, filled with whipped cream and rolled like a crepe.

Blintz Batter:
2 eggs
1 tablespoon butter, melted
1 ounce semisweet chocolate, melted
1 cup plus 2 tablespoons milk
½ teaspoon vanilla extract
1 cup flour
¼ cup sugar
Dash of cinnamon
Dash of salt

Filling:
1¼ cups cottage cheese, drained
1 tablespoon powdered sugar
¼ teaspoon vanilla extract
⅛ teaspoon cinnamon
¼ cup Raspberry Sauce (see below)

Raspberry Sauce:
3 cups fresh or frozen "dry pack" raspberries, thawed
½ cup unsweetened apple juice
⅛ to ¼ cup sugar
1½ teaspoons lemon juice
1 teaspoon cornstarch

For Blintz Batter: Place all ingredients in a blender and blend on highest speed for 20 to 30 seconds.

Pour ¼ cup batter per blintz into a non-stick crepe or frying pan. Swirl until the bottom of the pan is coated and pour off any excess batter. Cook on medium-high until top dries, then forms beads of

moisture. Flip blintz and cook just a few seconds on the other side. Remove blintz from pan and cool. Repeat until all the batter is used, making 3 blintzes.

For Filling: In a blender, blend all ingredients until thoroughly mixed. Set aside.

For Raspberry Sauce: In a blender, combine berries and apple juice. Blend until smooth. Add sugar to taste and blend again. Press mixture through a sieve to remove seeds.

In a saucepan, mix lemon juice and cornstarch until smooth. Add berry mixture and stir constantly over medium-high heat until sauce thickens and becomes clear. Remove from heat.

To Assemble: Preheat oven to 350 degrees. Place up to 2 tablespoons of the filling in the center of each blintz. Fold in the two sides, then the ends, so the blintz is square. Place 3 tablespoons of remaining Raspberry Sauce on the bottom of an ovenproof plate. Place the blintz, seam side down, on top of the sauce. Repeat so there are two blintzes per plate. Top with ¼ cup Raspberry Sauce.

Place plates in the oven for 10 to 12 minutes, watching carefully so that edges of sauce do not burn. Remove from oven and serve immediately, warning guests about the hot plates!

Makes 4 servings

In 1828, C.J. van Houten alkalized cocoa powder, making Dutch process cocoa powder. This was the first time since perhaps 600 A.D. that the once-bitter drink was sweetened to something similar to what we know as "hot chocolate" today.

Dark Chocolate Waffles

Not too sweet, these deep chocolate waffles can be topped with a variety of sweetened whipped cream and a variety of fruits or syrups, and they'd double as dessert fare. Innkeeper Carol Redenbaugh prefers them dusted with powdered sugar and crowned with fresh strawberries.

½ cup butter, melted
¼ cup sugar
2 eggs, separated
½ teaspoon vanilla extract
3 ounces bittersweet chocolate, melted and cooled
1½ cups flour
2 teaspoons baking powder
¼ teaspoon salt, optional
½ cup milk or ¾ cup buttermilk
Powdered sugar
Fresh strawberries, sliced and sweetened

Uno, dos, tres, cho-

Uno, dos, tres, -co-

Uno, dos, tres, -la-

Uno, dos, tres, -te

Bate, bate chocolate.

—Children's rhyme in Spanish

In the bowl of an electric mixer, beat butter and sugar. Add the egg yolks, vanilla and cooled chocolate. Mix well.

In a separate bowl, mix together the flour, baking powder and the optional salt. Add the flour mixture to the chocolate mixture alternately with the milk, blending well with each addition. (If using buttermilk, which is thicker than milk, add a little more, if necessary, to thin almost to a pouring consistency.)

With an electric mixer, beat the egg whites until stiff. Fold them into the batter.

Place about ⅓ cup batter in a hot waffle iron, close the cover and bake until the steaming stops; these waffles are dark so don't judge doneness by the color!

Serve sprinkled with powdered sugar and topped with strawberry slices.

Makes 5 to 6 waffles

The Graham B&B Inn and Adobe Village

With awesome red rock views from the pool or private balconies, guests at this award-winning inn almost hate to finish Carol Redenbaugh's gourmet breakfast to head for the hills. But Sedona's hiking amid the red rock formations and other attractions beckon, and later, guests love to retreat to their private room or casita, built of adobe. Carol and Roger strive to mix elegance and comfort at their inn.

The Graham B&B Inn
and Adobe Village
150 Canyon Circle Drive
Sedona, AZ 86351
800-228-1425
Fax 520-284-0767

Sea Crest by the Sea

Innkeepers Carol and John Kirby believe in delighting guests down to the smallest details, from an unusual chocolate entree at breakfast down to good reading lights in the 12 guestrooms. They entered innkeeping as a second career and restored this 35-room mansion from top to bottom after they bought it in 1990.

Sea Crest by the Sea
19 Tuttle Avenue
Spring Lake, NJ 07762
800-803-9031
908-449-9031

Fudge Oven Souffle with Chocolate Sauce

Cooked partially on the stove and partially in the oven, this omelette/souffle is fudgy yet light, with just a hint of orange or raspberry flavor. The heavenly chocolate sauce can be saved (or just make extra!) for topping ice cream, chocolate cake or fresh fruit.

1 tablespoon butter
1 cup semisweet chocolate chips
4 eggs, separated
⅓ cup powdered sugar, plus extra for dusting
⅓ cup sour cream
1 tablespoon orange or raspberry liqueur

Preheat the oven to 325 degrees. Melt butter in a 10-inch non-stick skillet with an ovenproof handle (or cover a wooden handle with aluminum foil). Set aside.

Melt chocolate chips in a microwave-proof bowl by microwaving on medium-high for 25 second intervals, stirring after each, until smooth. Set aside to cool.

In large bowl of an electric mixer, beat egg whites until frothy. Gradually beat in powdered sugar. Continue to beat until stiff peaks form when beaters are lifted.

In a small bowl, mix sour cream, liqueur and egg yolks.

Stir egg yolk mixture into cooled chocolate chips. Then fold mixture into egg whites.

Spread in buttered skillet. Place pan over low heat and cook without stirring or otherwise disturbing for 5 minutes. Transfer skillet to oven and bake for 15 to 18 minutes or until a toothpick inserted into the center comes out clean.

Remove pan from oven and loosen edges. Place a serving platter over the skillet and invert. Sprinkle with powdered sugar. Serve warm, cut into wedges, and pass the Chocolate Sauce for topping.

Makes 6 servings

Chocolate a "junk food?" It contains Vitamin A, Phosphorus, Potassium, Calcium, Iron, Niacin, Protein and a little Thiamine (Vitamin B-1) and Riboflavin (B-2). It also contains Phenylethylamine, the same chemical that makes us euphoric when we are in love.

Chocolate Sauce

1 cup semisweet chocolate chips
⅔ cup heavy cream
2 tablespoons orange or raspberry liqueur

Place chips in a microwave-safe bowl and microwave on medium-high for 25-second intervals, stirring in between, until melted. Whisk in cream until smooth. Stir in liqueur just before serving. Serve slightly warm or chilled. To store, cover and refrigerate.

Overnight French Toast Puff

Black Dog Inn,
Estes Park, Colorado

Like other busy innkeepers, Jane Princehorn appreciates that most of this dish can be made the night before. While many variations of an overnight baked French toast are favorites at inns, this one surprises and pleases Black Dog guests with rich chocolate!

1 loaf white bread, 12 to 13 slices, crusts removed
2 cups skim milk, divided
1 cup semisweet chocolate chips
½ cup sugar
2 teaspoons vanilla extract
8 eggs
2 cups half 'n half

Topping:
¾ cup butter or margarine, very soft or melted
1⅓ cups brown sugar, packed
1 cup chopped walnuts
1 cup flaked coconut
3 tablespoons dark corn syrup
Whipped cream

Generously grease a 9 x 13-inch baking dish that is at least 2 inches high. Arrange trimmed bread slices on bottom of pan in 2 layers, until all bread is used.

In a small saucepan, heat 1 cup milk (do not boil), chips and sugar, stirring until chips are melted and sugar is dissolved. Stir in vanilla. Let cool.

In a large bowl, beat eggs, remaining milk and half 'n half. Mix chocolate mixture into egg mixture. Pour over bread slices. Cover pan tightly and refrigerate overnight. In the morning, preheat oven to 350 degrees.

For Topping: Mix butter, brown sugar, walnuts, coconut and dark corn syrup. Spread the topping over the bread slices.

Bake uncovered for about 1 hour or until the center is set. (If edges are browning too fast, cover with foil.) Remove from oven and cool for 10 minutes or so, until cool enough to spoon or slice. Top with whipped cream (or maple syrup, frozen vanilla yogurt and/or chocolate syrup).

Makes 8 to 10 rich servings

Black Dog Inn

Black Dog Inn guests are staying in one of Estes Park's earliest homes, built in 1910. With a fieldstone fireplace and views of the Estes Valley, the family and living rooms are a gathering place for guests. Jane and Pete Princehorn and their black dog, Sara, welcome guests to four guestrooms named for the surrounding mountain peaks.

Black Dog Inn
P.O. Box 4659
650 South St. Vrain
Estes Park, CO 80517
970-586-0374

The Half Penney Inn

The Half Penney, named after the original owner's livestock brand, is an historic B&B inn, behind which runs the Appalachian Trail. Just a short drive from Hanover, New Hampshire, or Woodstock, Vermont, the inn is smack dab in the middle of year 'round outdoor activities, including x-c skiing just out the front door. Gretchen and Bob Fairweather offer five guestrooms in a home that was one of Vermont's first farms.

The Half Penney Inn
Box 84, Handy Road
West Hartford, VT 05084
802-295-6082

White Chocolate Frittata with Raspberry Coulis

Innkeeper Gretchen Fairweather serves this as an unusual breakfast entree to rave reviews at the Half Penney. You need to be a white chocolate-lover to appreciate this one, though. Gretchen notes that "more is not better" in terms of the white "chocolate" (vanilla) chips.

For Raspberry Coulis:
1 quart fresh raspberries

For Frittata, per person:
2 eggs
Dash of half 'n half
1 tablespoon vanilla chips (also called white confection or white chocolate)
Butter or margarine
Powdered sugar

Make Raspberry Coulis first (if you've made it a day ahead and refrigerated it, bring it to room temperature): Rinse berries. Set a few aside for garnish. With water still clinging, put berries in a saucepan or pot with a tight-fitting lid. Cook berries over low heat, stirring occasionally, until berries form a sauce. For a smooth, seedless sauce, strain. Chill.

Beat eggs and half 'n half. Fold in white chips.

Melt enough butter or margarine to cover the bottom of an ovenproof frying pan (allow 2 inches in height because frittata will puff up). Pour in egg mixture and cook over medium heat. As the eggs set on the bottom, gently lift around the edges to allow uncooked egg to flow to the bottom. Where there is a little moisture left on the top, place pan under a preheated broiler until puffed and golden.

Spread Raspberry Coulis in a circle on a serving plate. Cut frittata into wedges and place on top of the sauce. Sprinkle with powdered sugar, garnish and serve immediately.

Breads &
Coffeecakes

The McCallum House

Nancy and Roger Danley have operated this former suffragist's home as a B&B since 1983, one of the first B&Bs to open in Texas. Now grown from one to five distinctive guestrooms, their inn is a popular destination for those visiting the University of Texas at Austin or Austin's many attractions.

The McCallum House
613 West 32nd Street
Austin, TX 78705
512-451-6744
Fax 512-451-4752

Apple Fudge Cake

Apples and cinnamon are a surprisingly good combination with chocolate in this coffeecake. While Innkeeper Nancy Danley likes to reduce the fat in her recipes, she doesn't skimp on chocolate taste—this cake is very fudgy, as its name implies.

2 eggs, beaten
¾ cup applesauce
1 cup brown sugar, packed
1 teaspoon vanilla extract
1 medium unpeeled, chopped apple
1¼ cups flour
⅓ cup cocoa
1½ teaspoons cinnamon
1 teaspoon baking powder
½ teaspoon baking soda
Powdered sugar

Preheat oven to 350 degrees. Grease a small Bundt pan or regular bread loaf pan.

In a large bowl, mix eggs, applesauce, brown sugar, vanilla and apple.

In a separate bowl, sift together flour, cocoa, cinnamon, baking powder and baking soda. Blend flour mixture into applesauce mixture just until all ingredients are moistened.

Pour batter into prepared pan. Bake for 25 to 30 minutes or until a toothpick inserted into the center comes out clean. Cool for 10 minutes before inverting cake onto serving plate. Dust with powdered sugar (or drizzle with a simple vanilla frosting or glaze) before serving.

Makes about 8 servings

Chocolate Bread Pudding

This is a very sweet bread pudding that Jane and Pete Princehorn serve their guests as part of a full breakfast. Because it's so sweet and it looks just luscious, with golden brown custardy-bread and melty chocolate chips, it makes an impressive dessert or brunch item.

2 cups half'n half
7 eggs, beaten
1 cup sugar
1 teaspoon vanilla extract
11 or 12 cups trimmed and cubed day-old white bread, sponge cake, leftover coffeecake (such as peach or apple) or English muffin bread
1 cup semisweet chocolate chips

Preheat oven to 400 degrees. Butter an 8- or 9-inch square pan or casserole dish. Find a baking pan into which the dish will fit.

In a large bowl, whisk together half'n half, eggs, sugar and vanilla. Pour in bread cubes and stir gently until all are coated with egg mixture. Let rest for 20 minutes.

Fold in chocolate chips. Pour mixture into the prepared pan. Put that pan into larger baking pan, and fill larger pan with hot water until water is about 1-inch deep around the bread pudding pan.

Bake for about 1 hour or until firm in the center. Remove from oven and serve warm or room temperature.

Makes 8 servings

Black Dog Inn

Situated amidst towering pine and aspen, this inn is only a footpath away from Estes Park restaurants and attractions. Jane and Pete Princehorn are happy to share their knowledge of hiking, skiing, snowshoeing or other activities in the Rocky Mountain National Park. They provide guests with everything from a delicious breakfast to storage for outdoor equipment.

Black Dog Inn
P.O. Box 4659
650 South St. Vrain
Estes Park, CO 80517
970-586-0374

Chocolate Icebox Rolls with Ginger Filling

Whether you use Innkeeper Françoise Roddy's unique crystallized ginger filling or opt for the old-fashioned cinnamon-sugar mixture found in traditional cinnamon rolls, this chocolate sweet dough is a divine inspiration. Françoise appreciates being able to refrigerate the rolls, ready to bake, overnight, in order to have freshly baked, hot rolls for Woods House guests. As might be expected, the fragrance of the baking rolls is intoxicating!

The Woods House B&B Inn, Ashland, Oregon

Sweet Rolls:
2 cups milk
2 packets active dry yeast
½ cup warm water (105 to 115 degrees)
⅔ cup sugar
⅓ cup vegetable oil
1 egg
1 teaspoon vanilla extract
5 to 6 cups flour, divided
½ cup cocoa
1 tablespoon baking powder
2 teaspoons salt

Filling:
½ cup sugar
½ cup finely chopped crystallized ginger
½ cup chopped pecans
2 ounces semisweet chocolate, grated (or miniature chips)
4 tablespoons butter, melted

Frosting:
1 cup powdered sugar
1 tablespoon milk
½ teaspoon rum extract
½ teaspoon vanilla extract

For the Sweet Rolls: Scald the milk and allow to cool.

In a small bowl, dissolve the yeast in warm water.

In a large bowl, mix sugar, oil, egg and vanilla. When milk has cooled, add it, then stir in the yeast.

Stir in 2 to 3 cups of the flour, cocoa, baking powder and salt, beating dough until smooth. Beat in enough of the rest of the flour to make dough non-sticky and easy to handle.

On a well-floured surface, knead dough until smooth and elastic, 8 to 10 minutes.

Place dough in a greased bowl and turn it around so the greased side of dough is up. Cover and allow to rise in a warm place until double in size, about 90 minutes. Dough is ready if an indentation is left after the dough is poked.

Meanwhile, make the Filling: Mix sugar, ginger, pecans and chocolate. Set aside.

Grease two 9 x 13-inch baking pans. Punch dough down and divide it in half.

On the floured surface, roll one half into a rectangle about 10 inches by 12 inches. Spread with half of the melted butter, then top with half the Filling. Roll up, beginning at the 12-inch side. Pinch the edge of the dough into the roll to seal.

Cut the roll into 12 slices about 1-inch thick. Place cut-side down, slightly apart, in one of the prepared pans. Cover tightly with aluminum foil (double-wrap with plastic wrap first, if you prefer).

Repeat with other half of dough and filling. Refrigerate at least 12 hours, but no longer than 48 hours.

In the morning, preheat oven to 350 degrees. Remove pans from refrigerator and bake for 25 to 30 minutes.

Meanwhile, make Frosting: Mix powdered sugar, milk and rum and vanilla extracts. Drizzle over warm rolls.

Makes 24 rolls, about 12 servings

The Woods House B&B Inn

Guests at the Woods House enjoy a half-acre of terraced English gardens while being only four blocks from Ashland's renown theaters, shops and restaurants. That's one of the reasons Françoise and Lester Roddy bought this 1908 Craftsman-style inn. Another is the six sunny guest rooms, which they've stocked with fine amenities. They aim to make travelers "feel like a personal friend, not just a paying guest."

The Woods House
B&B Inn
333 North Main Street
Ashland, OR 97520
541-488-1598
Fax 541-482-8027

Chocolate Raspberry Date Bread

Date-lovers will enjoy this unusual use of chocolate in a marvelous yeast roll.

Bread:
1 packet dry yeast
⅓ cup warm water (105 to 115 degrees)
3 cups flour
½ cup sugar
½ teaspoon salt
½ cup unsalted butter, cubed
2 large eggs, beaten
2 tablespoons milk
1 teaspoon vanilla extract

Filling:
1 cup finely chopped pecans or walnuts
1 cup chopped, pitted dates
½ cup brown sugar, packed
1 teaspoon cinnamon
1 10-ounce jar raspberry pure-fruit spread
1 tablespoon water
6 ounces semisweet chocolate, peeled, or ½ cup miniature chocolate chips

Also:
2 ounces semisweet chocolate, melted
Fresh raspberries

Princess Anne of Austria brought chocolate with her to France when she married Louis XIII of France in 1615, setting off a chocolate craze among the French.

For the Bread: In a small bowl, sprinkle yeast over the water and let dissolve.

In a large bowl, mix flour, sugar and salt. Cut in cubes of butter with a pastry blender. Make a "well" in the center. Pour in yeast, eggs, milk and vanilla and stir until well combined and sticky.

Let dough rest for 2 minutes while you prepare a floured surface and rolling pin. Also, butter a large cookie sheet and two 9-inch long loaf pans.

Turn dough out onto floured surface and knead for 2 minutes with floured hands. Roll dough into a rectangle ¾-inch thick. Place on cookie sheet. Cover with plastic wrap and refrigerate while making filling.

For the Filling: Mix nuts, dates, brown sugar and cinnamon.

In a separate bowl, mix fruit spread and water until smooth.

Place dough back on floured surface and roll into a rectangle measuring 18 inches by 12 or 14 inches. Spread dough with raspberry mixture, leaving 1-inch border along one of the 18-inch long edges. Sprinkle date mixture evenly over the raspberry spread, then sprinkle with chocolate.

Moisten the 1-inch border edge with water. Starting at the other 18-inch edge, roll the dough up jelly roll-style. Cut the dough in half and place one 9-inch length in each of the prepared pans. (You can also cut the dough into 18 1-inch wide rolls, place them with one cut-side up in well-greased muffin cups as you would for cinnamon rolls, and bake for 15 to 20 minutes. Serve warm but be careful—filling stays hot!)

Let loaves rest for 10 minutes while preheating oven to 350 degrees. Bake about 50 minutes or until loaves are golden brown. Cool in the pan for 15 minutes, then remove to a rack. Cool 1 hour before slicing. Serve drizzled with melted semisweet chocolate and fresh raspberries.

Makes 18 servings

Breakfast in Willow Brook Inn's Teddy Bear Dining Room

The Willow Brook Inn Bed & Breakfast

Breakfast is served in the sun room or the dining room, decorated with teddy bears, at the Van Lenten's four-guestroom B&B. Originally built in 1929, this restored Arts & Crafts-style bungalow is now a hideaway for guests on an acre of wooded grounds. Yet guests are only 45 minutes from Detroit, 15 minutes from Detroit Metro airport, and 20 minutes from Ann Arbor, home of the University of Michigan.

Willow Brook Inn
Bed & Breakfast
44255 Warren Road
Canton, MI 48187
313-451-0019

Rancho San Gregorio,
San Gregorio,
California

Chocolate Zucchini Cake

You (and most of Lee and Bud Raynor's guests) won't guess there is organically-grown zucchini in this moist cake. The Raynors serve it as a coffeecake, though it would surely be appropriate for a dessert or snack cake.

½ cup milk
½ teaspoon lemon juice
½ cup butter or margarine
½ cup vegetable oil
1¾ cups sugar
2 eggs
1 teaspoon vanilla extract
2½ cups flour
¼ cup cocoa
1 teaspoon baking soda
1 teaspoon salt
½ teaspoon baking powder
½ teaspoon ground cloves
2 cups fresh shredded zucchini
¾ cup semisweet chocolate chips
¾ cup chopped nuts
Powdered sugar, whipped cream or mascarpone cheese

Preheat oven to 325 degrees. Grease and flour a 9 x 13-inch pan.

Mix milk and lemon juice and let stand for 5 minutes. Meanwhile, with an electric mixer, cream butter or margarine. Beat in oil, sugar, eggs and vanilla. Beat soured milk into creamed mixture.

In a separate bowl, stir together the flour, cocoa, baking soda, salt, baking powder and cloves. Stir the flour mixture into the butter mixture just until all ingredients are combined. Do not overmix. Fold the zucchini, chips and nuts into the batter by hand.

Spread batter into prepared pan. Bake for about 45 minutes or until a toothpick or knife inserted into the center comes out clean.

Serve warm or room temperature, cut into squares and dusted with powdered sugar or topped with a dollop of cream or mascarpone.

Makes about 24 squares

Rancho San Gregorio

Bountiful harvest breakfasts often feature produce from Lee and Bud Raynor's garden and apple orchard, part of their 15 creekside acres open for exploration by guests. The early California Mission-style inn has views of the coastal valleys and wooded hills only 10 miles from Half Moon Bay, less than an hour's drive from San Francisco. The Raynors offer four guestrooms with friendly hospitality and travel assistance.

Rancho San Gregorio
Route 1, Box 54
5086 La Honda Road
San Gregorio, CA 94074
415-747-0810
Fax 415-747-0184

French Chocolate Coffeecake

Yum! The bitter chocolate is tempered with sugar and the sweetness of the coffeecake itself. Like Innkeepers Carol and John Kirby, you'll make this one over and over.

½ cup butter, softened
½ cup butter-flavored shortening or margarine
1½ cups sugar
5 eggs
1 teaspoon vanilla extract
3 cups flour
2 teaspoons baking powder
1 teaspoon baking soda
1 cup sour cream

Topping:
½ cup sugar
1 teaspoon cinnamon
2 ounces unsweetened baking chocolate, grated
Powdered sugar

Preheat oven to 350 degrees. Grease a 10- or 12-inch tube pan or Bundt pan.

In large bowl of an electric mixer, cream butter, shortening and sugar. Beat in eggs, one at a time. Then beat in vanilla.

In a separate bowl, sift together flour, baking powder and baking soda. Add flour mixture to butter mixture alternately with the sour cream. Mix well.

For the Topping: In a small bowl, mix sugar, cinnamon and grated chocolate.

Put one-third to one-half of the thick batter in the bottom of the prepared pan. Sprinkle batter with half the topping. Repeat with the rest of the batter and topping. Run a knife through the topping and batter once to marble-ize the cake.

Bake about 55 minutes or until a toothpick or knife inserted into the center comes out clean. Cool pan for 10 minutes or more before inverting on a serving plate. Dust with powdered sugar before serving.

Makes 12 to 16 servings

Christmas at Sea Crest by the Sea

Sea Crest by the Sea

Breakfast at this inn is served at "the civilized hour" of 9:00 A.M. and often includes something unique, such as this coffeecake. Innkeepers Carol and John Kirby bought this three-story inn after a long search for just the right inn along the New Jersey coast. Located a block from the ocean, nine of the 12 guestrooms have ocean views, and all have beautiful amenities.

Sea Crest by the Sea
19 Tuttle Avenue
Spring Lake, NJ 07762
800-803-9031
908-449-9031

Mandarin Orange Chocolate Coffeecake

This recipe by Diane Kelley of Marysville, Washington, won the North Garden Inn's Breakfast Decadence recipe contest. No wonder—it's a hearty, filling coffeecake with an unusual but delicious combination of flavors.

2 eggs, lightly beaten
1 cup freshly squeezed orange juice
2 teaspoons vanilla extract
3 cups flour
1 cup sugar
1 tablespoon baking powder
1 teaspoon baking soda
1 teaspoon salt, optional
⅓ cup solid vegetable shortening, chilled and cut into ½-inch cubes
5 tablespoons unsalted butter, chilled and cut into ½-inch cubes
2 11-ounce cans mandarin orange segments, drained
1 cup semisweet chocolate chips

Topping:
1 cup sweetened flaked coconut
½ cup sugar
1 tablespoon butter, melted

Preheat the oven to 375 degrees. Butter and flour a 9 x 13-inch baking pan. (You can line the bottom of the pan with buttered parchment or waxed paper if you wish to invert the coffeecake and then re-invert it to a serving platter.)

In a small bowl, mix eggs, orange juice and vanilla.

In a large bowl, stir together the flour, sugar, baking powder, baking soda and salt. Using a pastry blender or your fingers, blend the shortening and butter cubes into the flour mixture until the mixture resembles coarse meal.

Make a "well" in the center of the flour mixture. With a wooden

spoon, stir the egg mixture into the flour mixture until all ingredients are combined and moist. With a rubber spatula, gently fold in the orange segments and chocolate chips.

Pour batter into the prepared pan and smooth the top.

For the Topping: In a medium bowl, mix coconut, sugar and butter. Sprinkle the topping over the coffeecake batter.

Bake for 35 to 45 minutes or until a toothpick inserted in the center comes out clean. Serve warm.

Makes about 24 servings

North Garden Inn

"Chocolate is an essential ingredient here at North Garden Inn," says Innkeeper Barb DeFreytas. So is music; the 10 guestroom B&B doubles as a studio for Barbara's husband, Frank, a music and voice teacher, and guests may use the Steinway grand piano in the sitting room. Their 1897 Queen Anne Victorian overlooks Bellingham Bay and is just 90 miles north of Seattle.

North Garden Inn
1014 North Garden
Bellingham, WA 98225
800-922-6414
206-671-7828

MapleHedge B&B Inn

Joan DeBrine found this early 18th-century Federal-style home after two-and-a-half years of searching for the perfect B&B, her long-time passion. She and her husband, Dick, offer five antique-filled guestrooms for travelers visiting April through December. The home, located in Charlestown's National Historic District, took the DeBrines another two-and-a-half years to restore and furnish before opening in 1990.

MapleHedge B&B Inn
355 Main Street
Charlestown, NH 03603
1-800-9-MAPLE-9
Fax 603-826-5237

MapleHedge Hungarian Coffeecake

Surprisingly delicious for such a short list of ingredients. Plus, it can feed a crowd and is good served warm or cold.

1 cup butter or margarine
1½ cups sugar
4 eggs, separated
3 cups flour
3 teaspoons baking powder
1 cup milk

Filling:
½ cup sugar
1½ tablespoons cocoa
1 teaspoon cinnamon

Preheat oven to 350 degrees. Grease a large tube or Bundt pan.

In large bowl of an electric mixer, cream butter. Blend in sugar and egg yolks.

In a separate bowl, mix flour and baking powder. Add to the butter mixture alternately with the milk.

In a separate bowl, beat egg whites until stiff. Fold into the batter.

For the Filling: In a small bowl or measuring cup, mix sugar, cocoa and cinnamon for topping.

Spread one-third of the batter on the bottom of the prepared pan. Sprinkle with one-third of the Filling. Repeat twice with other two-thirds of batter and Filling, sprinkling the last addition of Filling on top of the batter as a topping.

Bake for 55 minutes or until a toothpick or knife inserted into the middle of the cake comes out clean. Cool pan for at least 10 minutes before inverting cake and placing on a serving plate. Serve warm or room temperature. Cover tightly when cooled.

Makes 12 to 16 servings

Mocha Supreme Coffeecake

This recipe may have been the one that put the "coffee" into "coffeecake." The chocolate chips are a great addition, too, of course!

2 eggs
1½ cups milk
2 tablespoons butter, melted
3 cups flour
1 cup sugar
2 teaspoons baking powder
1 cup semisweet chocolate chips
1 to 2 tablespoons instant coffee powder

Crumb Topping:
6 tablespoons flour
4 tablespoons brown sugar, packed
4 tablespoons powdered sugar
2 to 3 tablespoons butter or margarine
1 teaspoon cinnamon

Preheat oven to 375 degrees. Grease and flour a 9 x 13-inch pan.

In large bowl of an electric mixer, beat together eggs, milk and butter. Beat in flour, sugar and baking powder. Stir in chocolate chips by hand. Stir in instant coffee powder by hand, just until it is blended into the batter (four strokes or less).

Spread dough in the prepared pan.

For Crumb Topping: In a small bowl, mix flour, brown sugar, powdered sugar, butter and cinnamon with a pastry blender, fork or clean hands. (Add more butter if necessary to make mixture hold together in crumbs.) Sprinkle over batter.

Bake for 25 to 30 minutes or until a toothpick inserted in the center comes out clean. Cool in pan for 10 minutes before cutting into squares and serving.

Makes about 24 servings

BonnyNook Inn

Breakfasts are served by candlelight in the formal dining room of this 1880's mansion, built during the cotton boom and now listed on the National Register of Historic Places. Bonny and Vaughn Franks "retired" into a career as innkeepers and caterers in Waxahachie, known for its concentration of gingerbread-trimmed homes. The Frankses also run an inn, Etta's Place, in downtown Fort Worth's Sundance Square.

BonnyNook Inn
414 West Main
Waxahachie, TX 75165
214-938-7202
800-486-5936

Toasted Walnut Fudge Bread

Toast yourself to a slice of this bread and it's like indulging in a warm brownie for breakfast.

1 cup coarsely chopped walnuts
3 ounces semisweet chocolate, melted and cooled
1 cup butter
1 cup sugar
5 eggs
2¼ cups flour
1 teaspoon baking soda
1 teaspoon salt
1 cup buttermilk
1 teaspoon vanilla extract

Preheat oven to 350 degrees. Grease two 9 x 5-inch loaf pans.

Spread walnuts on a baking sheet. Toast at 350 degrees for 3 to 5 minutes or until fragrant. Cool.

Melt chocolate in a microwave-proof dish by microwaving on medium high for 25 second intervals, stirring in between, until smooth. Cool.

With an electric mixer, cream butter and sugar. Beat in eggs one at a time. Mix in cooled chocolate.

In a separate bowl, mix flour, baking soda and salt.

Stir buttermilk and vanilla together. Add flour and buttermilk alternately to chocolate mixture. Stir in walnuts.

Divide batter between the two prepared pans. Bake for 55 to 60 minutes, or until a knife or toothpick inserted in the center comes out clean. Cool bread in pans for 10 minutes, then remove from pan and cool on a wire rack. Serve warm or toasted with butter.

Makes 2 loaves

The Willow Brook Inn Bed & Breakfast

Homemade breads and pastries are always featured at Bernadette and Michael Van Lenten's retreat, located on a wooded acre through which the Willow Brook wanders. Guests can feed the ducks and enjoy the gardens while still being close to major Detroit-area attractions, such as the Henry Ford Museum and Greenfield Village.

Willow Brook Inn B&B
44255 Warren Road
Canton, MI 48187
313-454-0019

Muffins, Scones & Popovers

Sea Crest by the Sea

A basket of freshly baked scones and muffins is part of the breakfast buffet at this inn, served from an antique sideboard. Guests enjoy a leisurely breakfast before a day at the beach or boardwalk in Spring Lake, near where John and Carol Kirby summered for years before becoming innkeepers. The inn has 12 carefully-decorated guestrooms among its 35 rooms.

Sea Crest by the Sea
19 Tuttle Avenue
Spring Lake, NJ 07762
800-803-9031
908-449-9031

Banana Chip Scones

Banana and peanut butter flavors blend with chocolate for wonderful, unusual scones.

- 2 cups flour
- ½ cup dark brown sugar, firmly packed
- 2 teaspoons baking powder
- ½ teaspoon baking soda
- ¼ teaspoon salt
- ¼ cup unsalted butter, chilled and cut into ½-inch cubes
- ¾ cup mashed ripe banana (1 large banana)
- 1 egg
- 3 to 4 tablespoons buttermilk
- 1 teaspoon vanilla extract
- ¾ cup peanut butter chips
- ¾ cup semisweet chocolate chips

Preheat oven to 400 degrees. Lightly grease a 10-inch diameter circle in the center of a baking sheet.

In a large bowl, stir together flour, brown sugar, baking powder, baking soda and salt. With a pastry blender, cut in the butter until the mixture resembles coarse crumbs.

In a small bowl, stir together the banana, egg, buttermilk and vanilla. Mix the banana mixture into the flour mixture. Stir in the two kinds of chips. Dough will be thick and sticky.

Spread dough into an 8- or 9-inch diameter circle in the center of prepared baking sheet. With a serrated knife, cut dough into 8 wedges.

Bake for 19 to 21 minutes, or until lightly browned and a toothpick inserted into the center comes out clean. Remove the baking sheet to a wire rack and cool for 5 minutes.

Recut into wedges, if necessary, and transfer with a spatula to a wire rack to cool, or serve warm. Store in an airtight container.

Makes 8 scones

Banana Chocolate Chip Muffins

Using miniature chocolate chips "allows the banana flavor to come through," said Innkeeper Marguerite Swanson, who never gets anything but compliments on these muffins. She serves them warm with butter.

2 very ripe large bananas
2 eggs
1 cup brown sugar, packed
½ cup margarine or butter, melted
1 teaspoon vanilla extract
2¼ cups flour
2 teaspoons baking powder
½ teaspoon cinnamon
½ teaspoon salt
¾ cup miniature semisweet chocolate chips
½ cup chopped nuts, such as walnuts

Preheat oven to 350 degrees. Butter or line 12 muffin cups.

Mash bananas or purée them in a blender.

In a medium bowl, mix bananas, eggs, sugar, butter and vanilla. Set aside.

In a large bowl, combine flour, baking powder, cinnamon and salt. Pour banana mixture into the flour mixture, stirring only until all ingredients are combined and moist. Fold in chips and nuts.

Fill prepared muffin tins three-quarters full. Bake for about 20 minutes or until a toothpick inserted into the middle comes out clean. Serve warm with butter.

Makes 12 muffins

Angel Arbor B&B Inn

From the angel statue to the vine-covered arbor, the innkeepers at this B&B pay attention to the tiniest detail. After six months of careful restoration, Marguerite and Dean Swanson opened this three guest-room inn for guests who appreciate hospitality and the convenience of being five minutes from downtown Houston.

Angel Arbor B&B Inn
848 Heights Boulevard
Houston, TX 77007
713-868-4654

Black Bottom Muffins

Rich and cheesecake-like, these could be served for dessert or tea, as well. Whenever you serve them, expect to impress family or friends, because they are wonderful. But don't overbake them or the cream cheese topping will be dry.

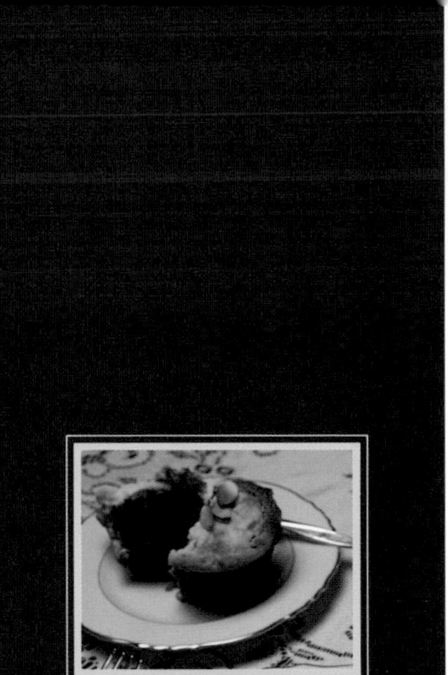

"One cup of this precious drinnk allows a man to walk a whole day without taking nourishment."
– Spaniard Hernán Cortés, introduced to chocolate by the Aztecs in 1519

¾ cup semisweet chocolate, chopped, or chips
⅓ cup butter
1¾ cups flour
1 teaspoon baking soda
½ teaspoon salt
½ cup buttermilk
½ cup sugar
1 egg, lightly beaten
1½ teaspoons vanilla extract

Topping:
12 ounces (1½ packages) cream cheese, softened
½ cup sugar
1 tablespoon flour
1 egg, lightly beaten
⅛ teaspoon almond extract
½ cup toasted, slivered almonds, divided

Preheat oven to 375 degrees. Butter 12 muffins cups (paper liners are not recommended).

In a glass bowl, melt chocolate and butter by microwaving on medium high for 25 second intervals, and stirring each time until smooth. Cool.

While that mixture is cooling, mix flour, soda and salt in a large bowl. Set aside.

Meanwhile, make the Topping: In a bowl of an electric mixer, beat together the cream cheese, sugar, flour, egg and almond extract. Stir in ¼ cup almonds by hand. Set aside.

In a small bowl, whisk together cooled chocolate/butter, buttermilk, sugar, egg and vanilla.

In the large bowl with the flour mixture, stir in chocolate mixture. Then spoon chocolate batter evenly into muffin cups. Top with the cream cheese topping. Sprinkle remaining ¼ cup almonds on top.

Bake for 20 to 25 minutes or until a knife inserted into the center comes out with no chocolate "cake" batter; the top of the cream cheese layer may crack slightly, but it should still be white. Serve cool.

Makes 12 muffins

Victorian Treasure B&B Inn

Kimberly and Todd Seidl prepare a decadent "from scratch" breakfast everyday, served to their guests in the formal dining room of their 1897 Bissell Mansion. Guests can choose accommodations in two Queen Anne Victorians with extraordinary architectural details and antique-appointed rooms. The other home, the 1893 Palmer House, features romantic suites with fireplaces and whirlpools.

Victorian Treasure
B&B Inn
115 Prairie Street
Lodi, WI 53555
608-592-5199
800-859-5199

MapleHedge B&B Inn

Located in the heart of the Connecticut River Valley, this historic 18th-century home needed restoration and a loving touch when prospective innkeeper Joan DeBrine found it and saw in it her future B&B. Two-and-a-half years later, she opened a five-guestroom inn, which she and her husband, Dick, operate as a new career after Dick's retirement. After a fortifying breakfast, Joan can direct guests to the best local antiquing — she acquired many of the B&B's antique furnishings in the area.

MapleHedge B&B Inn
355 Main Street
Charlestown, NH 03603
1-800-9-MAPLE-9
Fax 603-826-5237

Buttermilk Orange Scones

Orange and chocolate are a great combination, and these scones are wonderful served warm (no butter needed).

2 cups flour
⅓ cup sugar
1½ teaspoons baking powder
½ teaspoon baking soda
6 tablespoons butter or margarine
¾ cup miniature semisweet chocolate chips
½ cup buttermilk
1 tablespoon freshly grated orange rind (rind from nearly 1 whole orange)
1 egg
1 teaspoon vanilla extract

Preheat oven to 400 degrees.

In a large bowl, stir together flour, sugar, baking powder and baking soda. With a pastry cutter, cut in butter until mixture resembles coarse crumbs. Stir in chocolate chips.

In a separate bowl, whisk together buttermilk, orange peel, egg and vanilla extract. Stir buttermilk mixture into flour mixture.

Pat dough into an 8- or 9-inch diameter circle on a lightly greased insulated cookie sheet. Score into 8 wedges with a serrated knife.

Bake for 20 minutes or until a toothpick inserted into the center comes out clean. Remove from the baking sheet and cool on a wire rack for 5 minutes. Recut wedges and serve warm or cool.

Makes 8 scones

Chocolate Chip Orange Scones

Flaky and buttery. It's hard to stop with just one! If desired, brush the tops of the scones with a glaze of 1 tablespoon orange juice and 2 tablespoons sugar.

2 cups flour
⅓ cup sugar
2 teaspoons baking powder
½ cup butter, chilled
2 eggs
¼ cup orange juice
1 teaspoon vanilla extract
½ teaspoon freshly grated orange peel
¼ cup miniature semisweet chocolate chips or chopped regular-sized chips

Preheat oven to 425 degrees. Butter an insulated cookie sheet.

In a large bowl, mix the flour, sugar and baking powder. With a pastry blender or fork, cut in the butter until the mixture resembles coarse meal.

In a small bowl, whisk together the eggs, juice, vanilla and orange peel. Stir the egg mixture and chocolate chips into the flour mixture with a fork.

Turn dough out onto a floured board and knead gently about 10 times, until it forms a cohesive dough. Roll dough out to a ½-inch thickness. Cut out scones with a well-floured cookie cutter.

Place scones fairly close together on the cookie sheet. Bake for 12 to 15 minutes, until lightly browned or a toothpick inserted in the center comes out clean. Allow scones to cool on the cookie sheet for 5 minutes before removing with a spatula.

Makes about 14 2- to 3-inch scones

The Woods House B&B Inn

The address is close to Ashland's Shakespearean theater, but the lush terraced gardens on a half-acre mean peace and relaxation for guests. Françoise and Lester Roddy enjoy cooking and creating new taste treats for their guests, as well as producing murder mystery weekends and workshops for aspiring innkeepers and hosting intimate garden weddings.

The Woods House B&B Inn
333 North Main Street
Ashland, OR 97520
541-488-1598
Fax 541-482-8027

Chocolate Lover's Muffins

"We love the richness of this muffin, especially with bittersweet chocolate," said Innkeeper Jerry Phillips. With cocoa powder, chocolate liqueur and chocolate pieces, they're a triple chocolate threat! Warm, they're irresistible; cool, they are like fudgy brownies.

2 eggs
½ cup vegetable oil
½ cup chocolate liqueur
¾ to 1 cup buttermilk
1½ cups flour
1 cup sugar
½ cup cocoa
2½ tablespoons baking powder
1 cup semisweet chocolate chips or bittersweet pieces (about 1 4-ounce bittersweet bar, chopped in the food processor or grated)

Emperor Montezuma II was said to have drunk more than 50 cups of *xocoatl* (the Aztec version of hot chocolate) every day, all in golden goblets which he threw into the lake outside his palace when he was finished. Montezuma believed the beverage, which he drank mixed with spices and sweetened with honey, to be a strong aphrodisiac.

Preheat oven to 350 degrees. Grease or line 12 tor 13 muffin cups.

In a medium-sized bowl, whisk together eggs, oil, liqueur and buttermilk.

In a large bowl, mix flour, sugar, cocoa, baking powder and chips or pieces. Pour the milk mixture into the flour mixture and mix well. If mixture is very thick, add a little more buttermilk (but batter will be thicker than cake batter, for instance).

Divide batter between 12 or 13 muffin cups. Bake for about 20 minutes or until a toothpick inserted in the center comes out clean. Remove from oven and cool muffins in pans for 5 minutes. Remove muffins from pans and serve immediately.

Makes 12 to 13 muffins

The Old Rittenhouse Inn

Indulgence is the name of the game in the Rittenhouse dining room, renown as one of the Midwest's finest gourmet restaurants. Guests in this grand old Queen Anne or at one of the Rittenhouse's three other properties nearby are treated to a decadent breakfast in the Victorian dining rooms. Bayfield is the gateway to the Apostle Islands National Lakeshore and offers a variety of outdoor activities.

The Old Rittenhouse Inn
301 Rittenhouse Avenue
Bayfield, WI 54814
715-779-5111

"Chocolate is not only pleasant of taste but it is also a veritable balm of the mouth, for the maintaining of all glands and humours in a good state of health. Thus it is, that all who drink it, possess a sweet breath."
–Dr. Stephani Blancardi, written in Amsterdam in the early 1700s

Chocolate Macadamia Muffins

Deep, dark, fudgy, yummy and versatile—these muffins are easily adapted to whatever nuts or chips you have on hand.

2 cups flour
1 cup sugar
¾ cup cocoa
2 teaspoons baking powder
1 teaspoon baking soda
¼ teaspoon salt, optional
1 cup semisweet chocolate chips, miniature chips or vanilla chips
½ cup chopped macadamia nuts
1 cup milk or buttermilk
⅓ cup vegetable oil
2 eggs, beaten
1 teaspoon vanilla extract

Preheat oven to 350 degrees. Grease or line 18 muffin cups.

In a large bowl, mix flour, sugar, cocoa, baking powder, baking soda, optional salt, chips and nuts.

In a smaller bowl, mix milk, oil, eggs and vanilla. Pour the milk mixture into the flour mixture. Stir only until all ingredients are combined and moist.

Fill muffin cups three-quarters full. Bake for 20 minutes or until a toothpick inserted in the center comes out clean. Remove from the oven and serve warm.

Makes about 18 muffins

Grandma's House B&B

Marilyn Farver has been accused of starting a five-guestroom B&B in the 1860 brick farmhouse just so she can cook "from-scratch" breakfasts, which she loves. She and her husband, David, restored and redecorated the original family farmhouse for their B&B. Guests can still meet farm animals, walk in the woods, or just relax on the porch, all just 50 miles from Cleveland in the heart of Wayne County farm country.

Grandma's House B&B
5598 Chippewa Road
Orrville, OH 44667
216-682-5112

Chocolate Popovers

Fill these crispy popovers with whipped cream or the Bavarian Cream listed on page 20. At Thorwood and Rosewood Inns, which specialize in romantic getaways, these popovers are always on the Valentine's breakfast menu.

3 eggs
1 cup milk
1 tablespoon butter, melted
1 cup flour
2 tablespoons shaved chocolate
¼ teaspoon salt

Preheat oven to 375 degrees. Heavily grease 12 non-stick muffin cups or 6 non-stick popover pans.

In a medium bowl, whisk or beat together eggs, milk and butter. Add flour, shaved chocolate and salt and beat until smooth.

Divide batter between the 12 cups, filling about three-quarters full. Bake for 45 to 50 minutes or until puffed and crispy on top. Remove from oven and serve as soon as possible. If you like, garnish with chocolate curls and strawberries.

Makes 6 huge or 12 medium popovers

Thorwood and Rosewood Inns

Often named most romantic getaways, this pair of historic inns have been lavishly appointed with unique fireplaces and whirlpools in every guestroom. Veteran Innkeepers Pam and Dick Thorsen restored Thorwood, a former steamboat captain's home, as one of Minnesota's first B&Bs, then did the same with Rosewood. Located just 30 minutes from the Twin Cities, the inns are in an historic Mississippi River town.

Thorwood and
Rosewood Inns
315 Pine Street
Hastings, MN 55033
612-437-3297
Fax 612-437-7796

Double Chocolate Almond Muffins

Innkeeper Judy Hotchkiss adds a little almond extract for a breakfast favorite at the Oakwood House. Almond-lovers will swear by this one.

¼ cup margarine or butter
1/3 cup plus 2 tablespoons sugar
2 eggs
¾ cup milk
1 teaspoon almond extract
1 teaspoon vanilla extract
1½ cups flour
½ cup cocoa
1 tablespoon baking powder
¼ teaspoon salt
½ cup miniature semisweet chocolate chips

Preheat oven to 425 degrees. Spray 14 muffin cups with non-stick cooking spray.

Place margarine or butter in a glass bowl and microwave for 20 or 30 seconds to soften. Mix in sugar with a rubber spatula. Whisk in eggs, milk, almond and vanilla extracts.

In a separate bowl, sift together flour, cocoa, baking powder and salt. Mix milk mixture into flour mixture, stirring just until all ingredients are combined. Then stir in chocolate chips.

Fill muffin cups three-quarters full. Bake for about 15 minutes or until a toothpick inserted in the center comes out clean. Remove from oven and let sit a few minutes before taking muffins from pan. Serve muffins warm with butter.

Makes 14 muffins

Oakwood House B&B

Oakwood House is a 1911 two-story home located just two miles from downtown Atlanta in the city's restored Inman Park historic area. Judy and Robert Hotchkiss have lived next door since 1978 and have watched the home go through a succession of uses, then enjoyed turning it into a home-away-from-home for guests. Guests find the small inn is close to the subway and restaurants, and they find Inman Park a delight to explore.

Oakwood House B&B
951 Edgewood Ave. NE
Atlanta, GA 30307
404-521-9320

The Inn at Merridun

Peggy and Jim Waller welcome guests to Merridun, an antebellum mansion surrounded by nine acres of shady oaks and century-old magnolias. Built in 1855–57, the plantation at one time included 8,000 acres, with cotton as the main industry. Peggy and Jim chose Union for their retirement and this historic mansion for a one-of-a-kind inn and restoration project.

The Inn at Merridun
100 Merridun Place
Union, SC 29379
864-427-7052

Double Chocolate Banana Muffins

Rich, moist muffins with a hint of banana. Your cardiologist might not appreciate them, but Peggy and Jim Waller's guests sure gobble them up!

¼ cup butter, softened
⅔ cup sugar
1 egg
⅔ cup sour cream
1 teaspoon vanilla extract
1 cup flour
2 tablespoons cocoa
½ teaspoon baking powder
½ teaspoon baking soda
Pinch of salt
1 ripe banana, mashed
½ cup semisweet chocolate chips
¼ cup coarsely chopped walnuts

Preheat oven to 350 degrees. Grease or line 10 to 12 muffin cups.

In a large bowl, mix butter, sugar, egg, sour cream and vanilla. Add flour, cocoa, baking powder, baking soda and salt all at once. Mix just until all ingredients are blended. Stir in mashed banana, chips and walnuts.

Fill muffin cups two-thirds to three-quarters full. Bake for 18 to 20 minutes or until a toothpick inserted into the center comes out clean (unless you hit a melted chocolate chip!). Cool for 5 minutes, then remove the muffins from the tins and place them on a rack. Serve warm or at room temperature.

Makes 10 to 12 muffins

Espresso Chip Muffins

"These muffins freeze well," notes Innkeeper and Baker Nadine "Dinie" Silnutzer. But there are rarely any leftover to freeze!

2 cups flour
½ cup sugar
2½ teaspoons baking powder
2 teaspoons instant espresso powder (or 4 teaspoons instant coffee powder)
½ teaspoon salt, optional
½ teaspoon cinnamon
1 cup milk, scalded and cooled
½ cup butter, melted and cooled
1 egg, lightly beaten
1 teaspoon vanilla extract
¾ cup miniature semisweet chocolate chips

Preheat oven to 375 degrees. Prepare 12 muffin cups.

In a large bowl, stir together flour, sugar, baking powder, espresso or coffee powder, optional salt and cinnamon.

In a separate bowl, mix milk (it must be cooled or it will melt the chocolate chips!), butter, egg and vanilla. Make a "well" in the center of the flour mixture. Pour in milk mixture and stir just until all ingredients are combined. Fold in chocolate chips.

Divide batter between 12 muffin cups. Bake 15 to 20 minutes or until a toothpick inserted in the center comes out clean.

Makes 12 muffins

Wedgwood Collection of Historic Inns

Three 19th-century homes on more than two acres of landscaped grounds make up the Wedgwood Collection, owned and operated by Carl Glassman and Dinie Silnutzer. The inns, with six guestrooms each, are in the historic district of New Hope, just steps from the village center of this Bucks County rivertown.

Wedgwood Inns
111 West Bridge Street
New Hope, PA 18938
215-862-2520
Fax 215-862-2570

Chocolate Cherry Muffins

Door County, Wisconsin, is famous for its tart cherry crop. The Inn at Cedar Crossing in Sturgeon Bay takes full advantage of the local specialty all year 'round, using frozen fruit. These rich chocolate muffins would be good even without the cherries!

2½ cups flour
1 cup plus 2 tablespoons sugar, divided
½ cup plus 2 tablespoons cocoa
2 teaspoons baking powder
1 teaspoon baking soda
1 teaspoon salt
¾ cup butter
2 eggs, beaten
About 1 cup milk
1 cup semisweet chocolate chips
2 cups frozen presweetened tart cherries, thawed and drained

Preheat oven to 350 degrees. Grease or line 18 muffin cups.

In a large bowl, mix flour, 1 cup sugar, cocoa, baking powder, baking soda and salt. Cut in the butter with a pastry blender.

Measure the beaten eggs, then add enough milk to make 1½ cups total liquid. Stir milk and eggs into flour mixture. Then add chips and cherries, stirring only until all ingredients are combined.

Fill muffin cups almost full. Sprinkle remaining sugar on top of muffins. Bake for 20 to 30 minutes or until a toothpick inserted in the middle comes out clean. If using greased muffin tins, allow muffins to cool almost completely before removing.

Makes 16 to 18 muffins

Inn at Cedar Crossing, Sturgeon Bay, Wisconsin

The Inn at Cedar Crossing

The guestrooms in this historic downtown mercantile building are upstairs, above Innkeeper Terry Wulf's acclaimed restaurant. Terry opened the inn first, replacing second floor apartments with nine sumptuous antique-filled guestrooms. Their popularity led to opening the restaurant, which specializes in fresh, regional foods and spectacular desserts.

The Inn at
Cedar Crossing
336 Louisiana Street
Sturgeon Bay, WI 54235
414-743-4200
Fax 414-743-4422

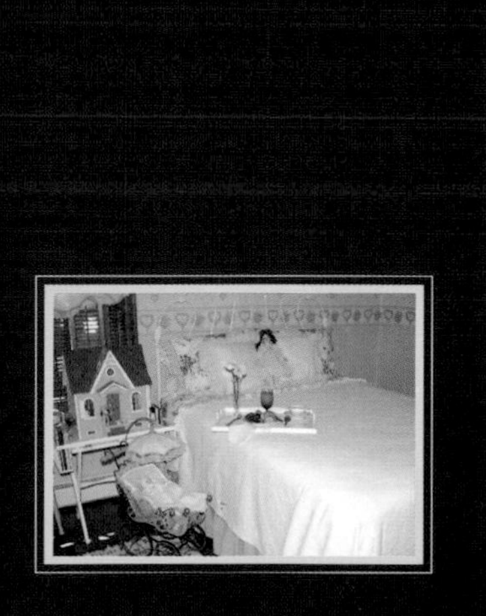

A welcoming bedroom at The Willow Brook Inn B&B, Canton, Michigan

A 1½ ounce chocolate bar contains about 9 milligrams of caffeine, compared to 150 mgs in a cup of coffee or 65 mgs in a 12-ounce soda pop.

Double Chocolate Delight Muffins

Brownie-like, these muffins seem best served with milk. Nuts, such as pecans or walnuts, are a good addition. Innkeeper Bernadette Van Lenten may serve these muffins along with afternoon tea.

3 ounces unsweetened chocolate
1 cup sugar
½ cup unsalted butter, softened
2 eggs
½ cup sour cream
½ cup milk
2 cups flour
¾ teaspoon baking powder
½ teaspoon baking soda
½ teaspoon salt
1 12-ounce bag semisweet chocolate chips (or vanilla chips)

Preheat oven to 375 degrees. Spray 6 giant-sized muffin cups or 12 regular cups with non-stick cooking spray.

In a microwave-safe bowl, melt chocolate in the microwave on medium-high for 25 second intervals, stirring in between until smooth. Set aside.

In a large bowl of an electric mixer, cream sugar and butter. Beat in eggs, then add sour cream and milk.

In a small bowl, stir together flour, baking powder, baking soda and salt. Pour flour mixture into butter mixture and stir together by hand. Stir in melted chocolate, then chocolate chips.

Fill muffins cups three-quarters full. Bake for about 20 minutes for standard-sized muffins or 25 minutes for giant muffins, or until a toothpick inserted into the center comes out clean.

Makes 6 giant or 12 standard muffins

The Willow Brook Inn Bed & Breakfast

Bernadette and Michael Van Lenten pamper guests at their 1929 Arts and Crafts-style home. They opened their four guestroom B&B after they enjoyed the pampering at many other B&Bs and dreamt of their own. The Willow Brook winds through their secluded property, and guests are welcome to feed the ducks or relax in the hammock.

Willow Brook Inn
Bed & Breakfast
44355 Warren Road
Canton, MI 48187
313-454-0019

Low-Cholesterol Double Chocolate Muffins

With no dairy products and no eggs, these muffins are just the ticket for diet-conscious guests at Rancho San Gregorio. For larger muffins, divide the batter among 10 cups instead of 12.

Rancho San Gregorio, San Gregorio, California

½ cup orange juice
½ cup water
3 tablespoons vegetable oil
1 tablespoon vinegar
1 teaspoon vanilla extract
1½ cups flour
½ cup sugar
¼ cup cocoa
1 teaspoon baking soda
½ teaspoon salt
⅓ cup miniature semisweet chocolate chips
Powdered sugar

Preheat oven to 375 degrees. Line 10 or 12 muffin cups.

In a large bowl, whisk together orange juice, water, oil, vinegar and vanilla.

In a separate bowl, mix flour, sugar, cocoa, baking soda and salt. Stir flour mixture into juice mixture, just until all ingredients are moist. Fold in chips.

Fill muffin cups three-quarters full. Bake for 12 minutes or until a toothpick inserted in the center comes out clean. Remove muffin pan and cool on a rack for several minutes. Sprinkle tops with powdered sugar before serving muffins warm.

Makes 10 to 12 muffins

Rancho San Gregorio

A healthy, hearty "harvest breakfast feast" always features produce organically grown on some of the 15 acres surrounding this inn. Innkeepers Lee and Bud Raynor invite their guests to hike in their orchard, wade in the creek, play badminton or volleyball, or explore the land, originally part of an 1839 Spanish Land Grant. Nearby are sandy beaches of Half Moon Bay, redwood groves, recreational trails and bird and elephant seal sanctuaries.

Rancho San Gregorio
Route 1, Box 54
5086 La Honda Road
San Gregorio, CA 94074
415-747-0810
Fax 415-747-0184

The McCallum House

Innkeepers Nancy and Roger Danley welcome guests to their comfortable 1907 home, just blocks from the University of Texas-Austin. They have restored the home, designed by a leading suffragist and local school superintendent. The Danleys love Austin, a wonderful city close to the Texas Hill Country, and they're happy to help guests explore the area.

The McCallum House
613 West 32nd Street
Austin, TX 78705
512-451-6744
Fax 512-451-4752

Lower-Fat Banana Chunk Muffins

Guests at the McCallum House benefit from Innkeeper Nancy Danley's commitment to lower her intake of fat without sacrificing flavor. She suggests you put in ½ cup chocolate chips and add more to taste. Sliced bananas (instead of the usual mashed bananas) add a nice chunk of flavor to the muffins.

2 egg whites
¾ cup non-fat plain yogurt
½ cup unsweetened or "natural" applesauce
½ cup brown sugar, lightly packed
2 cups flour
1½ teaspoons cinnamon
1½ teaspoons baking powder
½ teaspoon baking soda
2 ripe bananas, thinly sliced
½ to 1 cup semisweet chocolate chips or miniature chips
3 tablespoons sugar

Preheat oven to 375 degrees. Grease or line 12 to 14 muffin cups.

In a large bowl, whisk together egg whites, yogurt, applesauce and brown sugar.

In a separate bowl, sift together flour, cinnamon, baking powder and baking soda. Blend flour mixture into egg white mixture, stirring only until all ingredients are moist. Fold in banana slices and chocolate chips.

Fill muffin cups three-quarters full. Sprinkle tops with sugar. Bake for 15 to 17 minutes or until a toothpick inserted in the center comes out clean. Remove from oven and cool about 5 minutes before serving.

Makes 12 to 14 muffins

Magnificent Miniature Muffins

With an unusual combination of ingredients, these mini muffins are some of the guests' favorites, said Innkeeper Nancy Showers. (Those who don't care for maraschino cherries could substitute dried cherries or snipped dried apricots.)

½ cup butter
1 cup sugar
2 eggs
1 medium very ripe banana, mashed
2 cups flour
1 teaspoon baking soda
¼ cup chopped pecans
¼ cup miniature chocolate chips
⅓ cup chopped maraschino cherries

Preheat oven to 350 degrees. Butter or use a non-stick spray to butter up to 45 miniature muffin cups.

Soften butter for 15 seconds in the microwave. Then cream with the sugar, beating until light and fluffy. Beat in eggs one at a time. Add mashed banana and beat well.

Sift flour and baking soda. Stir by hand into the banana mixture. Fold in pecans, chips and cherries.

Fill miniature muffin cups about three-quarters full. Bake for 15 to 20 minutes, or until a toothpick inserted into the center comes out clean. Remove from the oven and remove muffins from tins. Serve immediately or cool on a wire rack.

Makes about 45 miniature muffins

The Inn at Olde New Berlin

Located in the wooded hills and rolling farmlands of Central Pennsylvania, John and Nancy Shower's Inn at Olde New Berlin is widely acclaimed for its accommodations and dining in Gabriel's, their 50-seat restaurant. The Showers lovingly restored the turn-of-the-century home in this historic town of 900. The five guestrooms are decorated with period furnishings, and the restaurant features home-baked breads and desserts.

The Inn at
Olde New Berlin
321 Market Street
New Berlin, PA 17855
717-966-0321
Fax 717-966-9557

The Inn at Cedar Crossing

Innkeeper Terry Wulf left a banking career to open a nine-guestroom inn, reminiscent of a small, luxurious European hotel. Located in downtown Sturgeon Bay, the gateway to the Door County peninsula, the inn was immediately a hit, and an award-winning restaurant soon followed.

The Inn at
Cedar Crossing
336 Louisiana Street
Sturgeon Bay, WI 54235
414-743-4200
Fax 414-743-4422

Mocha Chocolate Chip Scones

Pastry Chef Jeanne Demer's scones are absolutely chock-full of chocolate chips and walnuts. Never skimping on the good stuff has paid off for Terry Wulf, who owns and operates this popular Door County, Wisconsin, inn and restaurant.

3 cups flour
½ cup plus 2 tablespoons sugar
1½ tablespoons baking powder
1½ teaspoons salt, optional
¾ cup butter
1½ cups semisweet chocolate chips
¾ cup chopped walnuts
1 tablespoon instant coffee powder or granules
1 tablespoon hot water
2 eggs
Milk

Preheat the oven to 350 degrees. Grease two insulated cookie sheets.

In a large bowl, combine flour, sugar, baking powder and optional salt. Cut in the butter with a pastry blender. Stir in chips and walnuts. Set aside.

In a separate bowl, dissolve coffee powder in hot water.

Slightly beat the two eggs. Place in a measuring cup and add milk to make 1 cup total liquid. Blend the coffee and egg mixture into the flour mixture. Stir only until all ingredients are combined and moist.

Turn dough out onto a floured surface. Knead about 8 or 10 times. Pat or roll dough out to a 1-inch thickness. Cut with a knife into 12 wedges or use a floured glass to cut 12 round scones. Place on the prepared cookie sheets.

Bake for 15 to 25 minutes or until golden brown on top. Remove from the oven and let stand 5 minutes, then serve immediately.

Makes 12 scones

Maria Theresa of Spain gave Louis XIV of France (Anne and Louis XII's son) chocolate as an engagement gift. When they married, she moved in with her *Molina*, a servant whose only job was to make (hot) chocolate for her boss. Someone once said about Maria Theresa, "Chocolate and the King are her only passions." (In that order?)

Mocha Walnut Chip Muffins

With a chocolate batter and chocolate chips, these coffee-flavored muffins are not for the timid. The inn's Wendy Kleinknecht developed this recipe especially for chocolate lovers.

2 cups flour
2 tablespoons cocoa
1 tablespoon baking powder
1 to 2 tablespoons instant espresso powder (double if using instant coffee powder)
½ cup sugar
¾ cup miniature semisweet chocolate chips
½ cup chopped walnuts
1 cup buttermilk
2 eggs
½ cup butter, melted

Preheat oven to 400 degrees. Grease or line 16 muffin cups.

In a large bowl, mix flour, cocoa, baking powder and coffee powder. Stir in sugar, chips and walnuts.

In a separate bowl, whisk together buttermilk, eggs and melted butter. Stir buttermilk mixture into flour mixture, mixing just until all ingredients are moistened.

Fill muffin tins about three-quarters full. Bake for 15 to 18 minutes, until springy to the touch or until a toothpick inserted into the center comes out clean (except for melted chocolate chips).

Makes about 16 muffins

White Swan Inn

Fresh-baked pastries are an important part of breakfast at all the elegant California inns in the Four Sisters Inns collection. The White Swan is a European-style 26-room hotel set in the heart of San Francisco. Next door is the French country–themed Petite Auberge. Both inns have inviting breakfast rooms and sitting areas with fireplaces to enjoy breakfast and afternoon tea.

White Swan Inn
Four Sisters Inns
845 Bush Street
San Francisco, CA
94108
415-775-1755
800-999-9570

Sea Crest by the Sea

Guests enjoy indulging in the richness of this muffin as well as the richness of this elegant inn, and most come to indulge themselves on a getaway from a fast-paced life. Carol and John Kirby, who left busy careers for innkeeping, try to create a comfortable ambiance in their restored inn, located one block from the ocean. The Kirbys aim to turn first-time guests into repeaters, and they offer 12 guestrooms to please a variety of tastes.

Sea Crest by the Sea
19 Tuttle Avenue
Spring Lake, NJ 07762
800-803-9031
908-449-9031

Raspberry Chocolate Chip Muffins

Quick, easy and delicious. If these muffins are served warm, the chocolate chips are still all melty and there's no need for butter. (Reduce the milk to ¼ cup and you have a rich shortcake to be topped with more fresh berries and whipped cream.)

2 cups flour
¼ to ½ cup sugar, depending on taste
2½ teaspoons baking powder
½ teaspoon salt, optional
¼ teaspoon nutmeg
1 cup milk or buttermilk
½ cup butter, melted and cooled
1 egg, slightly beaten
1 cup fresh raspberries
¼ cup miniature semisweet chocolate chips
Powdered sugar

Preheat oven to 400 degrees. Grease 12 muffin cups.

In a large bowl, mix flour, sugar, baking powder, salt and nutmeg.

In a separate bowl, combine milk, butter and egg. Make a "well" in the middle of the flour mixture. Pour milk mixture into well and stir until all ingredients are combined and moist.

Fold in raspberries and chocolate chips with as few extra strokes as possible.

Divide batter evenly between 12 muffin tins. Bake 12 to 18 minutes, or until a toothpick inserted in the center comes out clean. Cool 5 minutes. Remove muffins to a wire rack to cool or serve warm. For a nice touch, dust with powdered sugar before serving.

Makes 12 muffins

Spicy Chocolate Pumpkin Muffins

If you've ever thought pumpkin pie could be vastly improved with some chocolate, these muffins are for you.

½ cup butter, softened
1 cup sugar
2 eggs
1 teaspoon vanilla extract
¾ cup solid pack canned pumpkin
1½ cups flour
1 teaspoon baking soda
1 teaspoon cinnamon
½ teaspoon salt
½ teaspoon nutmeg
½ teaspooon cloves
1 cup regular or miniature semisweet chocolate chips
½ cup chopped nuts

Preheat oven to 325 degrees. Grease or line 6 giant or 12 standard muffin cups.

In large bowl of an electric mixer, cream butter and sugar. Beat in eggs and vanilla. Then mix in pumpkin.

In a separate bowl, mix flour, baking soda, cinnamon, salt, nutmeg and cloves. Mix into creamed mixture. By hand, stir in chocolate chips and nuts.

Fill muffin tins three-quarters full. Bake for about 30 minutes (longer for giant ones) or until a toothpick inserted in the center comes out clean.

Makes 6 giant or 12 standard muffins

North Garden Inn

This 1897 Queen Anne Victorian, listed on the National Register of Historic Places, has 10 guestrooms, several of which offer views of Bellingham Bay. Barbara and Frank DeFreytas returned this apartment building to its former glory as a grand private residence and opened their B&B in 1986. Bellingham is ideally located for visitors to Vancouver, Seattle or the North Cascades National Park.

North Garden Inn
1014 North Garden
Bellingham, WA 98225
800-922-6414
206-671-7828

The Lamplighter B&B

Judy and Heinz Bertram welcome guests to their 1894 home, originally built as the home and office of a local surgeon. After living and traveling in Europe, the Bertrams brought their extensive collection of art and antiques to this well-appointed B&B, which features original woodwork and fireplace. Nearby, guests can enjoy the sandy beaches of Lake Michigan or biking, antiquing or exploring scenic western Michigan.

The Lamplighter B&B
602 East Ludington Ave.
Ludington, MI 49431
616-843-9792
Fax 616-845-6070

Spicy Mocha Apple Muffins

These moist muffins are an appealing and unusual combination of chocolate, coffee, apples and spices.

1½ cups flour
¾ cup sugar, plus ¼ cup for sprinkling on muffin tops
½ cup cocoa
1 tablespoon instant coffee powder or granules
2½ teaspoons baking powder
1 teaspoon cinnamon
Freshly grated nutmeg, to taste
1 egg
½ cup vegetable oil
½ cup milk
1 large apple, unpeeled, chopped
½ cup chopped nuts, optional

Preheat oven to 350 degrees.

In a large bowl, mix the flour, ¾ cup sugar, cocoa, coffee powder, baking powder, cinnamon and nutmeg.

In a separate bowl, whisk together the egg, oil and milk.

Combine the two mixtures in the larger bowl. Add the chopped apple and optional nuts, stirring only until well-combined.

Spoon into greased or lined muffin tins three-quarters full. Sprinkle tops of muffins with remaining sugar. Bake for 12 to 15 minutes.

Makes about 18 muffins

Desserts for Breakfast, Tea-Time & Snacks

Chocolate Apricot Torte

This chocolate-crusted treat is often on the decadent dessert menu at The Inn at Cedar Crossing, an award-winning historic inn and restaurant in Wisconsin's Door County. The chocolate-flecked crust is wonderful (if chopping chocolate is hard on your home food processor, use mini chips instead, or grate the chocolate by hand). Top with shaved chocolate curls or whipped cream.

Filling:
2 cups chopped, dried apricots
1½ cups water
½ cup sugar
3 tablespoons flour
2 tablespoons lemon juice

Crust:
½ cup chopped semisweet baking chocolate or miniature chocolate chips
2 cups finely chopped walnuts
1¾ cups flour
¾ cup brown sugar, packed
½ teaspoon salt
¾ cup butter
2 teaspoons vanilla extract

Preheat oven to 350 degrees. Grease and flour a 9-inch springform pan.

For Filling: In a medium saucepan, mix apricots, water, sugar, flour and lemon juice. Cook over medium-high heat, stirring constantly, until thick. Set aside to cool.

For Crust: Cut together chocolate, walnuts, flour, brown sugar, salt, butter and vanilla with a pastry blender. Press two-thirds to three-quarters of the crust mixture on the bottom and two-thirds of the way up the sides of the prepared pan. Pour filling into crust and smooth it out. Crumble remaining crust over top as streusel topping.

Bake for 25 minutes.

Makes 8 to 10 servings

The Inn at Cedar Crossing

Period antiques, cozy fireplaces, poster and canopy beds and down comforters are a part of each of the nine guestrooms in this historic downtown Sturgeon Bay inn. Innkeeper Terry Wulf turned second-floor apartments into lavish guestrooms, then opened a restaurant in the storefront downstairs a few years later. Her restaurant has been rated in the top 25 in the state, specializing in creative regional cuisine, "scratch" bakery and sinful desserts.

The Inn at
Cedar Crossing
336 Louisiana Street
Sturgeon Bay, WI 54235
414-743-4200
Fax 414-743-4422

Chocolate Cherry Bon-Bon Crepes

As if there was room for dessert after six other courses, these crepes are the finale at Bonny and Vaughn Franks' seven-course candlelight dinners. Somehow the guests seem to squeeze them in. And no wonder. The crepes are light, the ice cream refreshing, the cherries flavorful and the chocolate sauce . . . well, try it and see!

Crepes:
3 eggs
2 egg yolks
1 cup flour
Pinch of salt
1 cup milk
2 tablespoons vegetable oil
½ tablespoon sugar
1 to 2 teaspoons almond extract, optional

Cherry Sauce:
1 16-ounce can pitted tart cherries, drained (reserve liquid)
½ cup sugar
1 tablespoon cornstarch

Chocolate Sauce:
6 ounces semisweet chocolate
¼ cup sugar
⅓ cup butter
¼ cup heavy cream
¼ cup cherry liqueur

Also:
Vanilla ice cream
Sliced almonds, pecan pieces or extra tart cherries

The first milk chocolate bar was made in 1875 by two Swiss businessmen. Daniel Peter added baby food-maker Henrí Nestlé's sweetened-condensed milk to chocolate.

For Crepes: Place eggs, yolks, flour, salt, milk, oil, sugar and optional almond extract into blender. Blend for 1 minute on high. Scrape sides with a spatula and blend again until contents are smooth, about 30 seconds. If possible, refrigerate batter for 1 hour to reduce bubbles.

Heat an 8-inch non-stick skillet or electric crepe maker. Pour enough batter to cover the bottom. Cook until top dries and edges may curl slightly, then flip with a spatula and cook for just a few seconds on the other side.

Cool flat. Crepes may be frozen on a flat plate in a freezer bag.

For Cherry Sauce: Drain cherries, reserving the juice. Measure juice and add enough water to make 1 cup total liquid.

In a saucepan, mix sugar and cornstarch. Then stir in cherry juice. Cook over medium heat until sauce is thick, then boil for 1 minute. Reduce heat and stir in cherries. Keep warm on low heat.

For Chocolate Sauce: In the top of a double boiler or in a microwave-safe bowl, place chocolate, sugar, butter and cream. Microwave for 25 second intervals, stirring in between, or stir over moderate heat until chocolate and butter have melted. Whisk in cherry liqueur. Stir in a bit more heavy cream if necessary to thin.

To Assemble: Place a crepe on a dessert plate. Place one scoop of ice cream on half of the crepe. Top ice cream generously with cherry sauce. Fold the other half of the crepe over the ice cream and cherry sauce. Top with chocolate sauce, sprinkle with nuts or top with additional cherries and serve immediately.

Makes 7 to 8 crepes

BonnyNook Inn

Guests at this inn are treated to more than fine food by Bonny and Vaughn Franks. The innkeepers, who spent six years restoring this 1880s home as a B&B, are attentive hosts who know Waxahachie, 30 miles south of Dallas, well. For guests they offer candlelight breakfasts, a Victorian parlor with games and a grand piano, and specially arranged lunches and dinners.

BonnyNook Inn
414 West Main
Waxahachie, TX 75165
214-938-7202
800-486-5936

Garth Woodside Mansion
B&B Inn, Hannibal,
Missouri

Chocolate Heaven Logs

A new twist on an old favorite: chocolate chip cookies. The finished version, which can be quite elegant, still practically begs to be served with a glass of milk. Caution: the dough is wonderful and easy to overdose on!

¾ cup margarine, softened
¾ cup sugar
1 egg
1½ teaspoons vanilla extract
2¼ cups flour, sifted
½ teaspoon salt
6 ounces (⅞ cup) semisweet
  chocolate chips or miniature
  chips

Chocolate Coating:
6 ounces (⅞ cup) semisweet
  chocolate chips
2 tablespoons margarine
2 cups ground walnuts

Preheat oven to 350 degrees. Grease insulated cookie sheets.

In large bowl of an electric mixer, beat margarine, sugar, egg and vanilla until well-mixed.

In a separate bowl or on a sheet of waxed paper, sift together flour and salt. Blend flour into creamed mixture. Stir chips in by hand.

On a lightly floured surface, shape dough into "logs" about 2 inches long and ½ inch wide. Place on a greased cookie sheet. Bake for 12 to 15 minutes until cookies are set. Cool cookies on cookie sheet on wire racks. Meanwhile, prepare Chocolate Coating.

For Chocolate Coating: Melt chocolate and margarine in a double boiler or in a large glass measuring cup by microwaving and stirring every 15 to 25 seconds until smooth. If mixture is too thick, add a little melted margarine.

Dip ends of logs into chocolate, scraping the excess from the back of the cookie onto the side of the measuring cup. Roll or dip chocolate-coated ends in nuts. Place on waxed paper until set. Store covered in a single layer.

Makes about 32 (if you stay out of the dough)

Garth Woodside Mansion B&B Inn

This elaborate 1871 mansion was the summer home for Colonel John Garth, who held lumber and tobacco interests, and his family. Garth and his wife, Helen, were school chums of Samuel Clemens (Mark Twain), who was often a guest at their home. Innkeepers Irv and Diane Feinberg turned the mansion, set among 39 acres of woods and meadows, into a welcoming B&B. They recently opened Abigail's Secret, a romantic hideaway in Hannibal's historic district.

Garth Woodside Mansion
B&B Inn
R.R. 3, Box 578
Hannibal, MO 63401
573-221-2789

Chocolate-Glazed Shortbread "Doggie Bones"

Innkeeper Susan Sinclair cuts these rich shortbread cookies into doggie bone shapes as part of her dog Bailey's annual tea-time birthday bash. Bailey doesn't get to eat any, but the guests who celebrate with party hats and singing surely enjoy them! Those who prefer to cut them into other shapes may do so with Susan's and Bailey's blessing.

Shortbread:
1½ cups butter, softened
1 cup powdered sugar
1 tablespoon vanilla extract
3 cups flour

Glaze:
¼ cup heavy cream
1 cup (6 ounces) semisweet chocolate chips
2 teaspoons light corn syrup

Preheat the oven to 325 degrees.

In large bowl of an electric mixer, cream butter until smooth. Slowly blend in powdered sugar. Then beat in the vanilla. Add flour and mix until well blended.

Divide the dough in half. Flatten each piece into a disk and wrap in plastic wrap. Refrigerate until firm, about 90 minutes.

On a floured board using a floured rolling pin, roll the dough out to ⅛-inch thickness. (Turn dough often to prevent sticking.) Cut cookies out with cookie-cutters and place on ungreased insulated cookie sheets.

Bake for 16 to 18 minutes or until "set," but do not let cookies brown. Remove from oven and transfer cookies immediately to a cool flat surface.

Some Things Never to Do with Chocolate:

~ Give it to a dog (dogs can't digest it, and that can prove fatal)

~ Melt it the wrong way so it burns

~ Get water in it when melting

~ Leave it on the dashboard in the summer, especially in Phoenix

~ Share it with someone who doesn't really appreciate good chocolate.

Meanwhile, make Chocolate Glaze: In a small saucepan, scald the cream. Stir in chips and corn syrup and cover. Let stand off the heat for up to 15 minutes.

Gently whisk the glaze until smooth, being careful not to create bubbles.

Dip half of each "bone" cookie into the glaze. Transfer to a tray or cool cookie sheet covered with waxed paper. Chill cookies for 10 minutes in refrigerator to set. Store, covered, in refrigerator; serve cool or at room temperature.

Makes about 28 bones/cookies (depending on size of cookie cutter)

The Maples Inn

"Bailey the Wonder Dog," a miniature schnauzer, is the inn mascot at the Maples Inn, Susan Sinclair's restored 1903 home on a quiet Bar Harbor street. Bailey and Susan welcome guests with refreshments, served on the front porch or by the fire. The treats are enjoyed by guests returning from a day of hiking or biking Acadia National Park, only 5 minutes away, exploring the Maine coast, or shopping in Bar Harbor's many boutiques and galleries. Guests enjoy the friendly atmosphere of this inn, which was originally built to house wealthy summer guests to Mount Desert Island.

The Maples Inn
16 Roberts Avenue
Bar Harbor, ME 04609
207-288-3443

Angel Arbor B&B Inn,
Houston, Texas

Chocolate Rum Pound Cake with Fudge Glaze

This is a wonderfully rich and moist ganache-covered cake, which Innkeeper Marguerite Swanson serves often at weddings and special dinners. You'll want to use the shiny glaze on other cakes.

⅔ cup unsweetened cocoa, divided
¼ cup boiling water
1¼ cups butter or margarine, softened
2⅔ cups sugar
1 teaspoon vanilla extract
5 eggs
2 cups flour
1 teaspoon salt
½ teaspoon baking powder
¼ teaspoon baking soda
½ cup buttermilk
¾ cup finely chopped pecans
¼ cup light rum

Preheat oven to 325 degrees. Grease and flour a 12-cup Bundt pan.

In a small bowl or measuring cup, mix ⅓ cup cocoa and water until smooth. Set aside.

In large bowl of an electric mixer, beat butter, sugar and vanilla until creamy. Beat in eggs one at a time. Then stir in the cocoa and water mixture.

In a separate bowl, mix flour, remaining ⅓ cup cocoa, salt, baking powder and baking soda. Add flour mixture to butter mixture alternately with buttermilk, beating well after each addition. Mix in pecans and rum.

Pour batter into prepared pan. Bake for about 65 minutes or until a toothpick or knife inserted in the center comes out clean. Cool cake 10 minutes before inverting onto a serving plate. Frost with Fudge Glaze when completely cool.

Makes 12 to 16 servings

Fudge Glaze

- 3 tablespoons butter
- 3 tablespoons light corn syrup
- 1 tablespoon water
- 1 cup semisweet chocolate chips

In a small saucepan, stir butter, corn syrup and water constantly until mixture boils. Remove from heat and stir in chocolate chips until glaze is smooth.

Cool slightly before drizzling over cooled cake. (This is a thick glaze that firms up to a nice frosting; thin with a little hot water if preferred.)

Angel Arbor B&B Inn

Guests can go out and enjoy the garden here, or enjoy just looking at it from the year 'round solarium Innkeepers Marguerite and Dean Swanson built when they restored this 1923 brick home and opened it as a B&B in 1996. They enjoy pampering guests in their well-appointed historic inn, whether guests come for business or pleasure. Many guests come in groups of 12 to experience Marguerite's personally-written Murder Mystery dinners, known for both fun and food.

Angel Arbor B&B Inn
848 Heights Boulevard
Houston, TX 77007
713-868-4654

Christmas Brownie Alaska

Spectacular presentation is what Wedgwood Inns guests receive: Colorfully-layered ice cream under a blanket of meringue and sitting atop a truly Fudgy Brownie. Whether you use Innkeeper Carl Glassman's favorite combination of ice creams or your own—and whether you can keep your hands off the brownie when you make it ahead—is up to you!

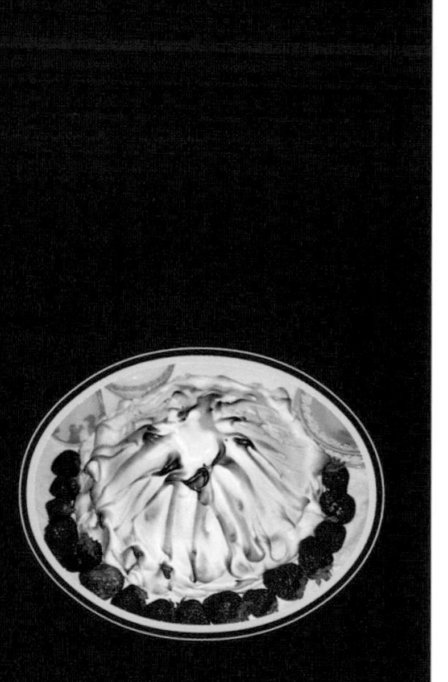

Four hundred cacao beans are needed to make 1 pound of chocolate.

1½ cups strawberry ice cream, softened
2 cups pistachio ice cream, softened
3 cups vanilla ice cream, softened
1 baked Fudgy Brownie layer (recipe below)
3 egg whites
⅓ teaspoon salt
¼ teaspoon cream of tartar
6 tablespoons sugar

A few hours or a day before preparing, soften ice creams and layer into a bowl as follows: In a deep 8-inch diameter mixing bowl, press strawberry ice cream into the bottom. Freeze until firm. Top strawberry layer with pistachio layer, freeze, then top with vanilla layer and freeze again.

Prepare Fudgy Brownie and cool. Unmold the three layers of ice cream onto the brownie layer (dip the bowl for a few seconds into a larger bowl containing hot water, if necessary, to loosen the ice cream). Return ice cream-topped brownie to freezer while preparing meringue.

Beat egg whites with salt and cream of tartar with an electric mixer until mixture is foamy throughout. Beat in sugar, 1 tablespoon at a time, and then continue beating egg whites on high speed until stiff peaks form.

Preheat oven to 450 degrees. Place one oven rack on bottom rung and remove other rack(s).

Cut brown Kraft paper in a 9-inch circle and place in center of baking sheet. Place ice cream-topped brownie in center of paper. Cover with meringue, sealing completely down to the brown paper. Place in oven for up to 6 minutes or until meringue is golden brown.

Remove from oven and transfer paper circle to a 10-inch or larger serving plate and serve at once. Cut in pie-shaped slices.

Makes 8 to 10 servings

Fudgy Brownie

2 ounces unsweetened chocolate
⅓ cup butter
2 eggs
1 cup sugar
1 teaspoon vanilla extract
⅔ cup flour
½ teaspoon baking powder
¼ teaspoon salt
½ cup chopped pecans or walnuts

Preheat oven to 350 degrees. Generously grease an 8-inch round cake pan, then line with waxed paper.

Melt chocolate with butter in saucepan over very low heat, stirring constantly until smooth (or melt in a microwave-proof dish by heating on medium high for 25 second intervals, stirring in between each heating). Remove from heat.

With an electric mixer, beat eggs thoroughly. Blend in sugar. Beat in chocolate mixture. Add vanilla and beat again.

In a separate bowl or measuring cup, mix flour, baking powder and salt. Stir flour mixture into chocolate mixture. Stir in nuts by hand.

Pour batter into prepared pan. Bake for 25 to 30 minutes or until a toothpick inserted in the center comes out clean. Remove from oven and cool pan for 10 minutes. Then remove brownie from the pan, remove waxed paper and finish cooling on a wire rack.

Wedgwood Collection of Historic Inns

Wedgwood Inn, Umplebe House and Aaron Burr House are the three Bucks County inns to which this ambitious husband-and-wife team welcome travelers. Dinie Silnutzer and Carl Glassman's adjacent inns offer garden gazebos, picnic tables and a game of croquet at tea-time, or, in the winter, a cozy parlor fire and conversation. From fresh-baked pastries at breakfast to homemade almond liqueur before bed, indulging their guests has been their top priority since opening in 1981.

Wedgwood Inns
111 West Bridge Street
New Hope, PA 18938
215-862-2520
Fax 215-862-2570

Cook's Double Chocolate Rebels

Cocoa makes the batter chocolate and chocolate chips make the cookies yummy; oatmeal makes them sort-of nutty. Make this recipe once and you'll make it again.

The Redwing B&B,
Ashland, Oregon

1½ cups sugar
1¼ cups butter-flavored shortening
¼ cup water
1 egg
1 teaspoon vanilla extract
½ teaspoon salt, optional
6 tablespoons cocoa
1 cup flour
½ teaspoon baking soda
3 cups quick-cooking rolled oats
1 12-ounce bag semisweet chocolate chips

Preheat oven to 350 degrees.

In large bowl of an electric mixer, cream sugar, shortening, water, egg and vanilla. Beat in optional salt and cocoa, then flour and baking soda. Mix well. Stir in oatmeal and chocolate chips (by hand, if you do not have a heavy duty mixer).

Drop in golf ball-sized balls on ungreased cookie sheets. Bake for 12 minutes or until small bubbles appear over the top of cookies. Cool cookies on the sheet for a few minutes before removing to cooling racks.

Makes 3½ dozen cookies

Cowboy Cookies

The taste of toasted coconut and pecans is a tasty surprise in these crispy chocolate chip cookies. Innkeeper Judi Cook notes she often varies the nuts to include Oregon filberts (hazelnuts), almonds, walnuts, pecans or a mixture of all those types.

1 cup flaked coconut
¾ cup chopped pecans
1 cup butter, softened
½ cup sugar
1½ cups brown sugar, packed
2 eggs
1½ teaspoons vanilla extract
2 cups flour
1 teaspoon baking soda
½ teaspoon salt
2 cups rolled oats (old-fashioned or quick-cooking)
2 cups semisweet chocolate chips

Preheat oven to 350 degrees. Grease insulated cookie sheets.

Spread coconut and pecans on a cookie sheet or jelly roll pan. Place in oven for 3 to 5 minutes. Stir and repeat toasting for another 3 to 5 minutes until coconut is thoroughly brown. Cool before adding to cookie mixture.

In large bowl of an electric mixer, cream butter and the two sugars. Add eggs and vanilla and beat well. Mix in flour, baking soda and salt. Stir in oats, chips and toasted coconut and pecans (by hand, if you do not have a heavy duty mixer).

Drop from a rounded teaspoon onto greased cookie sheets (these do not spread much).

Bake for 10 to 12 minutes or until browned.

Makes about 5 dozen cookies

The Redwing B&B

Innkeeper Judi Cook is indeed a great cook, creating memorable breakfasts for guests in her 1911 Craftsman-styled home. Cook, who also owns a specialty food business, always keeps her cookie jar stocked for guests coming or going from the Oregon Shakespeare Festival, located just a short walk away.

The Redwing B&B
115 North Main Street
Ashland, OR 97520
541-482-1807

Deep Dark Chocolate Fudge Cake

The Inn at Merridun, Union, South Carolina

Swedish botanist Linnaeus noted that the cocoa tree "supplies the raw product for a most delicious, healthy and nourishing drink." In 1753, he gave it its scientific name, theobroma cacoa. "Theobroma" means "food of the gods."

"For our overnight guests, as well as our luncheon and dinner guests, we always have at least two choices for dessert," said Innkeper Peggy Waller. "One is always chocolate." This very, very chocolate cake "is one of our guests' favorite desserts." A triple layer cake, this is impressive for birthdays or other special occasions.

2 eggs
1 cup milk
½ cup vegetable oil
2 teaspoons vanilla extract
2 cups sugar
1¾ cups flour
¾ cup cocoa
1½ teaspoons baking powder
1½ teaspoons baking soda
1 teaspoon salt, optional
1 cup boiling water

Preheat oven to 350 degrees. Grease and flour three 8- or 9-inch cake pans.

In large bowl of an electric mixer, beat eggs, milk, oil and vanilla. Beat in sugar, flour, cocoa, baking powder, baking soda and optional salt. Mix for 2 to 3 minutes. Stir in boiling water; batter will be very thin.

Pour batter into prepared pans. Bake for 30 to 35 minutes or until a toothpick inserted into the center comes out clean. Remove from oven and cool for 10 minutes. Then remove cakes from pans and cool completely before frosting.

Makes 12 to 16 servings

Chocolate Frosting

1 cup cocoa
¾ cup butter, melted
½ cup hot milk
4 cups powdered sugar
2 teaspoons vanilla extract

In large bowl of an electric mixer, beat cocoa with melted butter and hot milk. Add powdered sugar and vanilla and beat on medium speed until smooth and thick.

Cool to room temperature before frosting cake. Makes about 3 cups frosting.

The Inn at Merridun

Learn about the fascinating history of this 140-year-old antebellum mansion while enjoying a homemade chocolate treat on its 2,400 square feet of porches. While the massive inn, complete with elegant crystal chandeliers and a curved stairway, might seem overwhelming, Innkeepers Peggy and Jim Waller and J.D., the inn cat, put guests immediately at ease. They "retired" into innkeeping after medical careers in the Navy.

The Inn at Merridun
100 Merridun Place
Union, SC 29379
864-427-7052

The Inn on the Green

The Inn on the Green is, indeed, on a green—it is a white southern Colonial home on 10 acres overlooking a golf course. Shelley and Brad Jilek's B&B is quiet and scenic, and the woods out back are home to wild turkey and deer. Jileks did major work before opening with four guestrooms. Located in southern Minnesota's Bluff Country, the Inn on the Green is a half-hour drive from the Mississippi River and LaCrosse, Wisconsin.

The Inn on the Green
Rt. 1, Box 205
Caledonia, MN 55921
507-724-2818
Fax 507-724-5571

Easy Frozen Chocolate Mousse Cups

This easy frozen mousse is the perfect ending to a huge Inn on the Green breakfast, and it's made with pasteurized eggs to avoid any salmonella possibilities. Innkeeper Shelley Jilek says the mint flavor makes this the ultimate dessert.

- 1 cup butter, slightly softened
- 2 cups powdered sugar
- 4 ounces unsweetened chocolate, melted
- 1 cup pasteurized eggs or pasteurized egg substitute, to equal 4 eggs
- 1 teaspoon vanilla extract
- ¾ teaspoon peppermint extract, optional
- 1 cup vanilla wafer or chocolate-flavored vanilla wafer crumbs
- Whipped cream
- Maraschino cherries

With an electric mixer, beat butter and powdered sugar on high for several minutes, until fluffy. Beat in melted chocolate. Gradually add eggs and beat again until fluffy. Add extracts and mix well.

Spoon about ¼-inch deep wafer crumbs in the bottom of 18 cupcake liners (placed in a muffin tin).

Divide the mousse mixture evenly among the 18 cups. Freeze until firm. Remove from freezer just a few minutes before serving and top with a dollop of whipped cream and a maraschino cherry, if desired. Store covered in the freezer.

Makes 18 servings

Espresso Brownies

Ooh, boy, with sour cream, butter and eggs, these are the richest, moistest and best brownies ever. The coffee flavor makes them "adult" and the chocolate chips make them doubly sinful.

1 cup semisweet chocolate chips
½ cup butter
3 eggs
¾ cup sour cream
1 teaspoon vanilla extract
¼ cup vegetable oil
1¼ cups flour
1¾ cups sugar
½ cup cocoa
3 tablespoons instant espresso powder (or 5 tablespoons instant coffee powder)
½ teaspoon baking powder
½ teaspoon salt, optional
1½ cups chopped nuts (walnuts, pecans and/or almonds)

Preheat oven to 350 degrees. Butter a 9 x 13-inch baking pan.

Place chocolate chips and butter in a glass bowl and microwave on medium-high for 25 seconds. Stir and microwave again for 20 second intervals, stirring in between, until mixture is completely melted and smooth. Mix in eggs, sour cream, vanilla and oil.

In a separate large bowl, mix flour, sugar, cocoa, espresso or coffee powder, baking powder and optional salt. Stir chocolate mixture into flour mixture until all ingredients are thoroughly blended.

Spread batter into the prepared pan. Sprinkle nuts over top.

Bake on the center rack for 25 to 30 minutes or until a toothpick inserted into the center comes out clean. Remove from oven and cool completely before cutting.

Makes 24 large brownies

The Redwing B&B

Innkeepers Judi and Mike Cook searched for the perfect B&B in several Oregon communities before settling on Ashland. They found the Redwing, purchased it, redecorated inside and out, and opened their B&B with three guestrooms. It's located close to shops, restaurants and Shakespeare theaters.

The Redwing B&B
115 North Main Street
Ashland, OR 97520
541-482-1807

Country Garden Inn, Napa, California

In the mid-1700s, chocolate was first sold in the Colonies by apothecaries as a medicine. For more than two decades, other societies had been hailing chocolate's abilities for everything from strength, vigor and sexual prowess to settling upset stomachs.

Flourless Chocolate Torte

Let's face it, there's nothing in this recipe that's good for you, so if you're avoiding flour for health reasons, this torte won't help you much! Innkeeper Lisa Smith serves it simply because it tastes good. And it's pretty, topped with a minty cream cheese frosting and sprinkled with chocolate chips.

10 ounces semisweet chocolate
2 ounces unsweetened chocolate
¾ cup butter
8 eggs, separated
1 cup granulated sugar
1 tablespoon vanilla extract
Pinch of salt

Preheat oven to 350 degrees. Test large springform pan to make sure it does not leak if it sits in a water bath. If it does leak, line it with heavy duty aluminum foil, then spray the foil with a non-stick cooking spray. It if does not leak, spray the bottom, line it with parchment and then spray the parchment.

In a double boiler over hot water or in a large microwave-proof bowl, melt chocolates and butter (microwave on medium-high for 25 second intervals, stirring in between). Remove from heat and cool.

In large bowl of an electric mixer, beat the egg yolks and sugar on high speed until the mixture is thick and drops from the beaters in ribbons. Stir in vanilla and salt. When chocolate mixture is fairly cool, stir it into the egg yolk mixture.

In a separate mixing bowl, beat the egg whites until soft peaks form. Fold egg whites into chocolate mixture. Then pour into the prepared pan.

Set the pan in a large baking pan. Add 1 inch of water to the baking pan.

Bake for at least 50 minutes or until a toothpick inserted in the middle comes out clean, rotating pan every 15 minutes for even baking. Remove from oven and cool completely before removing sides and parchment/foil. When cool, frost with Mint Topping.

Makes about 14 servings

Mint Topping

2 ounces cream cheese
1½ teaspoons peppermint extract
3 cups powdered sugar
1 or 2 drops liquid food color, your choice
Semisweet chocolate chips

In a food processor, combine cream cheese, extract and powdered sugar. Process until the mixture forms a ball and is glossy. (Add 1 tablespoon water, if necessary.) Thin with a tablespoon of water at a time until the mint mixture is the consistency of yogurt. Add food coloring and process again.

Spread or drizzle mint topping over cooled torte (some mint topping may be left over), then sprinkle with chocolate chips.

Country Garden Inn

One reviewer called this "a B&B that puts as much effort into its culinary offerings as it does into its bedroom decor." Innkeepers Lisa and George Smith delight guests at the breakfast table and again at tea-time, after a day wine tasting, hiking, riding or otherwise exploring the Napa Valley. Guests also love the inn's circular rose garden and aviary, with up to 40 bird species.

Country Garden Inn
1815 Silverado Trail
Napa, CA 94558
707-255-1197
Fax 707-255-3112

Fudge Mound Cookies

These are soft "adult" chocolate cookies because of the hint of mocha in the frosting. If there are any left to store, leave them separate rather than stacking in the cookie jar, or they'll stick together (and then you'd have to eat the whole glob—terrible!) Worth making mashed potatoes to have the leftovers for this recipe!

1 cup mashed potatoes
¾ cup sugar
¾ cup brown sugar, packed
½ cup butter-flavored shortening
1 egg
1 teaspoon vanilla extract
2 cups flour
6 tablespoons unsweetened cocoa
2 teaspoons cinnamon
1 teaspoon baking powder
1 teaspoon baking soda
1 teaspoon salt
½ teaspoon nutmeg
½ cup milk

Preheat oven to 350 degrees. Grease insulated cookie sheets.

Cream potatoes, sugars, shortening, egg and vanilla.

In a separate bowl, mix the flour, cocoa, cinnamon, baking powder, baking soda, nutmeg and salt. Alternating with the milk, add the flour mixture to the creamed mixture.

Allow dough to stand for 10 minutes. Drop from a tablespoon at least 2 inches apart onto greased cookie sheets.

Bake for 12 to 15 minutes, until tops of cookies appear dry. Let cool thoroughly before frosting.

Makes up to 3 dozen cookies

Mocha Frosting

2 cups powdered sugar
3 to 4 teaspoons sweet cocoa
½ cup hot coffee, divided
½ teaspoon vanilla extract

Mix powdered sugar, cocoa, 4 tablespoons of the coffee and the vanilla. Thin to a spreading consistency with more coffee.

The Gosby House

Homemade cookies are always available at the Gosby House and the other romantic country inns in the collection owned by Roger and Sally Post and named for their four daughters. Located on the Monterey Peninsula, this inn has 22 sumptuous rooms in the main home and carriage house. The inn has been welcoming guests for more than 100 years. A shoreline path that winds its way along the rocky coast to the popular Monterey Aquarium begins just a few blocks away.

The Gosby House
Four Sisters Inns
643 Lighthouse Avenue
Pacific Grove, CA 93950
408-375-1287
Fax 408-655-9621

The Redwing B&B

Grandma Lulu must have passed down her love of chocolate and wonderful baked goods to Innkeeper Judi Cook. Judi not only cooks tempting breakfasts for guests but operates her own specialty food business, focusing on marvelous muffin mixes. Judi and her husband, Mike, offer three guestrooms in an historic Craftsman-style home.

The Redwing B&B
115 North Main Street
Ashland, OR 97520
541-482-1807

Grandma Lulu's Chocolate Pound Cake

Perfect summer-time treat topped with fresh raspberries or strawberries and whipped cream. In the winter, add sliced bananas or serve ala mode (add hot fudge sauce if you dare!).

6 ounces (⅞ cup) semisweet chocolate chips
½ cup boiling water
1 cup butter
2 cups sugar
4 eggs
1 teaspoon vanilla extract
2½ cups flour
1 teaspoon baking soda
½ teaspoon salt
1 cup buttermilk

Preheat oven to 350 degrees. Grease a large tube pan or Bundt pan.

Melt chocolate chips in boiling water, stirring until smooth.

In large bowl of an electric mixer, cream butter and sugar. Beat in eggs one at a time. Then beat in vanilla and melted chocolate.

In a separate bowl, sift together flour, baking soda and salt. Add flour mixture to chocolate mixture alternately with the buttermilk, scraping down the sides of the bowl after each addition.

Pour batter into tube pan and bake for up to 90 minutes, checking after 60 minutes with a knife or toothpick inserted in the center. Remove from oven when tester comes out clean.

Makes 12 to 16 servings

Heavenly Montana-Sized Chocolate Chip Cookies

These are the giant cookies you see in bakeries—but at Susan Ridder's B&B, they are offered for guests' snacks. Chewy with a nutty flavor extended by the oatmeal.

- 1 cup butter
- 1 cup sugar
- 1 cup dark brown sugar, packed
- 2 eggs
- 1 teaspoon vanilla extract
- 2 cups flour
- 1 teaspoon baking powder
- 1 teaspoon baking soda
- ½ teaspoon salt
- 2½ cups rolled oats (old-fashioned or quick-cooking)
- 1½ cups semisweet chocolate chips
- ½ cup chopped walnuts

Preheat oven to 325 degrees. Grease insulated cookie sheets.

In large bowl of a heavy duty electric mixer, cream butter and sugars. Beat in eggs and vanilla.

In a separate bowl, mix flour, baking powder, baking soda and salt. Beat it into creamed mixture. Mix in oats, chips and walnuts (by hand, if you do not have a heavy duty mixer).

With a ¼ cup measure, scoop out ¼ cup batter per cookie, placing 5 inches apart on greased cookie sheets. Bake for about 20 minutes or until top is dry and slightly cracked.

Makes 18 4-inch cookies

Good Medicine Lodge

After fortification at a hearty breakfast buffet, guests at this cedar lodge are off for a day at the ski slopes, trout streams, hiking and biking trails, or other favorite recreational pursuits in the Whitefish and Glacier National Park areas. Outdoor enthusiasts and Innkeepers Susan and Chris Ridder offer nine spacious guestrooms in this 6,000-square-foot lodge with mountain views. Guests can unwind in front of fireplaces or under the Big Sky in the outdoor spa.

Good Medicine Lodge
537 Wisconsin Avenue
P.O. Box 562
Whitefish, MT 59937
406-862-5488
Fax 406-862-5489

Hint of Mint Chocolate Torte

This moist single-layer cake is topped by a wonderful, shiny ganache and plenty of chocolate curls. Innkeeper Nancy Shower's slightly-mint dessert is also festooned with fresh mint and edible pansies, nasturtiums or rose petals. Even if you opt for the glaze-topping alone, this is still a spectacular dessert with just the right amount of mint.

Torte:
¾ cup sugar
¾ cup sour cream
½ cup butter, softened
1 egg
1 teaspoon vanilla extract
½ teaspoon peppermint extract
1 cup flour
¼ cup cocoa
½ teaspoon baking powder
½ teaspoon baking soda
¼ teaspoon salt, optional

Curls:
6 ounces semisweet chocolate

Glaze:
3 1-ounce squares semisweet chocolate
3 tablespoons butter
2 teaspoons light corn syrup
1 teaspoon vanilla extract
⅛ teaspoon peppermint extract

Also:
Powdered sugar

For the Torte: Preheat the oven to 350 degrees. Grease a 9-inch round cake pan. Line the bottom with parchment or waxed paper, then grease the parchment or waxed paper.

In a large bowl of an electric mixer, beat sugar, sour cream, butter, egg, and vanilla and peppermint extracts. Blend in flour, cocoa, baking powder, baking soda and optional salt.

Spoon batter into pan, spreading evenly. Bake 30 to 35 minutes or until a toothpick inserted in the center comes out clean. Cool cake in pan on a wire rack for 10 minutes. Then loosen cake from the edge of pan. Invert onto wire rack and peel off parchment or waxed paper. Turn right-side up and cool completely.

Meanwhile, make Chocolate Curls: Place chocolate in a microwave-safe bowl and microwave on medium-high for 25 second intervals, stirring in between, until melted and smooth. Pour onto 2 large cookie sheets, spreading evenly. Refrigerate until firm, about 10 minutes.

Place chocolate-covered cookie sheet on top of a damp cloth to prevent it from sliding. Holding a straight-edge knife at an angle, push the blade away from you, across the chocolate, to form long, thin curls. (If chocolate is too firm, let stand at room temperature for a few minutes until soft enough to form curls; if it's too soft, return to refrigerator.)

Transfer curls with a toothpick or spatula to another plate. Refrigerate until ready to use.

For Glaze: In a heavy saucepan, place semisweet chocolate, butter, corn syrup, and vanilla and peppermint extracts. Heat over low heat, stirring until mixture is melted and smooth. Remove from heat and stir frequently until glaze cools and thickens slightly.

Brush crumbs from cake. Place it on a wire rack set over waxed paper. Spoon glaze over cake, spreading over top and sides. Let stand at room temperature until glaze is firm, about 45 minutes.

Place cake on a cake plate and arrange chocolate curls on top. Decorate with fresh mint and fresh edible flowers. Sprinkle lightly with powdered sugar.

Makes 10 to 14 servings

The Inn at Olde New Berlin

Freshly baked desserts and pastries are part of the reason guests love Gabriel's, the intimate restaurant located in the parlors of the Inn. Nancy and John Showers made a career change after raising their three oldest children and bought this 100-year-old home, built as a summer retreat for a Philadelphia family. The Showerses completed major restoration in six months and now offer five guestrooms with Amish quilts and antiques.

The Inn at
Olde New Berlin
321 Market Street
New Berlin, PA 17855
717-966-0321
Fax 717-966-9557

Old-Fashioned Chocolate Chip Oatmeal Cookies

An old family recipe, these cookies are now a raid-the-cookie-jar favorite at The Graham B&B Inn in Sedona, Arizona.

1 cup butter-flavored shortening
¾ cup sugar
¾ cup dark brown sugar, packed
2 eggs
1 teaspoon vanilla extract
1½ cups flour
1 teaspoon baking soda
1 teaspoon salt, optional
2 cups rolled oats (old-fashioned or quick-cooking)
1 12-ounce bag semisweet chocolate chips

Preheat oven to 375 degrees. Grease insulated cookies sheets.

In large bowl of an electric mixer, blend shortening and sugars. Beat in eggs and vanilla.

In a separate bowl, mix flour, baking soda and optional salt. Add to egg mixture. Stir in oats and chips (by hand if you do not have a heavy duty mixer.)

Drop golf ball-sized cookies well apart onto the cookie sheets. Bake for 12 minutes.

Remove pans from oven and cool cookies for 5 minutes before removing from trays. Eat 'em right away (as though you had to be told . . .)!

Makes about 40 cookies

The Graham B&B Inn and Adobe Village

Carol and Roger Redenbaugh enjoy entertaining guests from all over the world who come to explore Sedona's scenic red rock country and find elegance and comfort at this inn. The popularity of the six unique guestrooms and outdoor pool and hot tub led the couple to expand, constructing authentic adobe cottages and decorating each individually.

The Graham B&B Inn
and Adobe Village
150 Canyon Circle Drive
Sedona, AZ 86351
800-228-1425
Fax 520-284-0767

Red Devil Mocha Cake

The Inn at Merridun

From 1855 until 1990, the comforts of this antebellum mansion were reserved for its owners. Peggy and Jim Waller restored it and now welcome guests to the elegant mansion. Merridun boasts a music room, parlor and library, plus 2400 square feet of porches, set off by corinthian columns and marble porticos.

The Inn at Merridun
100 Merridun Place
Union, SC 29379
864-427-7052

A really moist layer cake with a nice mocha flavor. Perfect for an adult birthday cake. The frosting thins out with extra coffee to a beautiful shiny glaze. "This cake is also great with coconut-pecan frosting," swear the innkeepers.

1 cup mayonnaise
1 cup sugar
1 cup cold coffee
2 teaspoons vanilla extract
2 cups flour
1/3 cup cocoa
2 teaspoons baking soda
Pinch of salt

Frosting:
3 cups powdered sugar
½ cup cocoa
3 tablespoons cold coffee, plus several teaspoons extra
1 teaspoon vanilla extract

Preheat oven to 350 degrees. Grease and flour two 8- or 9-inch round cake pans (or line 18 to 20 cupcake tins with paper liners).

In large bowl of an electric mixer, combine mayonnaise, sugar, coffee and vanilla. Mix in flour, cocoa, baking soda and salt.

Pour into prepared pans. Bake 25 to 30 minutes (about 18 minutes for cupcakes) or until a toothpick or knife inserted into the center comes out clean. Cool cakes 5 minutes in pan, then turn out onto wire racks and cool completely before frosting.

For Frosting: With an electric mixer, beat powdered sugar, cocoa, 3 tablespoons coffee and vanilla. Add more coffee by the teaspoonful while beating until smooth and creamy and good spreading consistency.

Makes 12 to 16 servings

Toffee Bars

These are rich and wonderful. Master Chef Alain Borel uses only fine Belgian chocolate, but if it's not available near you, semisweet will do. These are often a tea-time and holiday favorite at this French country inn.

1 cup unsalted butter
½ cup sugar
½ cup brown sugar, packed
1 egg yolk
1 teaspoon vanilla extract
1¾ cups flour
¾ cup chopped pecans
11 ounces dark Belgian chocolate, chopped very finely, or 1¾ cups semisweet chocolate chips

Preheat oven to 350 degrees. Grease a jelly roll pan or 10 x 13-inch pan.

In large bowl of an electric mixer, cream butter and sugars. Beat in egg yolk and vanilla. Beat in flour. Set dough aside.

Spread pecans in a single layer in an ungreased pan. Toast in the 350-degree oven for 5 minutes. Remove from oven and cool.

Spread dough evenly in prepared pan. Bake for 15 to 20 minutes, depending on the size of the pan.

Remove from the oven. Immediately top with chocolate. When chocolate is melted, spread over bars. Sprinkle with nuts (press in with a sheet of waxed paper, if desired, to keep nuts from falling off). With a sharp knife, score into squares while bars are still warm. Cut after cooling.

Makes 42 to 47 rich bars

L'Auberge Provencale

Recreated as a true inn of the South of France by Celeste and Alain Borel, L'Auberge Provencale offers 11 guestrooms and a bucolic setting in the hunt country of northern Virginia. Alain, a French master chef, creates four-diamond French cuisine for breakfasts and dinners, often using his home-grown vegetables, herbs and spices. The award-winning inn boasts elegant accommodations and is especially popular for romantic getaways.

L'Auberge Provencale
Route 340
P.O. Box 119
White Post, VA 22663
800-638-1702
540-837-1375

Chocolate Truffles

If you're one of those folks who can't keep their fingers out of the icing on the chocolate cake, you'll have trouble resisting these rich truffles. Guests at this acclaimed New Hampshire inn find Innkeeper Laura Simoes has placed the truffles in the guestroom as a thoughtful turn-down treat.

5 ounces unsweetened chocolate
½ cup unsalted butter, at room temperature
2½ cups powdered sugar
4 teaspoons hazelnut-flavored liqueur (or half 'n half plus ½ teaspoon vanilla extract)

Also:
Unsweetened cocoa
Paper or foil liners for miniature muffin cups

In a heavy sauce pan or double boiler, melt chocolate over low heat or over hot water, or, in a glass bowl, microwave on medium-high for 25-second intervals, stirring each time, until melted.

Remove from heat or microwave. Stir in butter, then sugar, alternating each. Add liqueur or half 'n half and vanilla. Mix well.

Roll into balls of desired size, usually about ¾-inch diameter. Place on a baking sheet and refrigerate to cool completely.

Roll cooled truffles in cocoa. Place each truffle into a paper or foil liner. Store covered in the refrigerator. Serve at room temperature.

Makes 30 to 40 truffles, depending on size

The Inn at Maplewood Farm

Laura and Jayme Simoes' picture-perfect New England farmhouse has welcomed visitors for 200 years. The hospitality continues today with food-writer and Innkeeper Laura's homemade breakfasts and other thoughtful touches in four guestrooms and throughout the inn. After a day of hiking, antiquing or exploring the picturesque backroads of New Hampshire, fall asleep listening to old-time radio programs, broadcast to vintage radios in the guestrooms from Jayme's transmitter.

The Inn at
Maplewood Farm
P.O. Box 1478
447 Center Road
Hillsborough, NH 03244
800-644-6695
603-464-4242

Kahlua Tea-Time Truffles

These truffles are always part of the menu for tea-times at Angel Arbor, whether for formal tea or private tea parties. Innkeeper Marguerite Swanson also serves them for afternoon or evening snacks for guests, and packs them in decorative tins for holiday giving. The white "confection" sets up nicely and is a very pretty contrast to the deep, dark chocolate truffle.

There are two varieties of cocoa beans: Criollo, which makes the highest quality chocolate and accounts for only 10 percent of the beans harvested, and Forastero, easier to grow and more disease resistant. All beans are grown within 20 degrees of the Equator. The "recipes" for the mix of the varieties of beans are carefully-guarded secrets of chocolatiers.

2 cups crumbs from dark chocolate cream-filled sandwich cookies (grind about 20 cookies in food processor)
½ cup powdered sugar
2 tablespoons unsweetened cocoa
2 tablespoons light corn syrup
⅓ cup coffee-flavored liqueur, such as Kahlua (or non-alcoholic truffles, ⅓ cup heavy cream and substitute instant coffee powder for part of the cocoa)
1 cup ground pecans
8 ounces white chocolate confection

Also:
Paper or foil liners for miniature muffin cups

In a medium bowl, stir together cookie crumbs, powdered sugar, cocoa, corn syrup, liqueur or cream, and pecans. Form mixture into a large ball. Wrap in plastic wrap and refrigerate for up to 1 hour.

Shape dough into 36 balls and place on a wire rack over a pan or cookie sheet lined with waxed paper. Refrigerate truffles while melting white chocolate.

Melt white chocolate in a glass bowl in the microwave on medium-high for 25 seconds, stir, and repeat until smooth.

Dip top half of each truffle into white chocolate. Replace truffle, chocolate side up, on rack over waxed paper.

Refrigerate until white chocolate is set. Place each truffle into a lined muffin cup. Store in a tightly covered container (keep refrigerated if cream was used).

Makes about 36 truffles

Angel Arbor B&B Inn

Romance and suspense are both specialties at this historic Houston Heights inn. Marguerite Swanson specializes in serving guests who visit for romantic honeymoons, anniversaries and bridal showers, as well as Murder Mystery dinners for 12, which she writes herself. She and husband Dean restored this lovely 1923 home and opened three guestrooms in 1996, after a decade of operating a larger B&B just down the street. Both the angel (a statue) and a vine-covered arbor are accessible to guests in the garden.

Angel Arbor B&B Inn
848 Heights Boulevard
Houston, TX 77007
713-868-4654

Inn on Summer Hill By the Sea

Guests are pampered at this country inn with ocean view rooms, canopy beds, whirlpool tubs and even a dessert du jour, served each evening in the cozy dining room. This 16-guestroom inn is situated amid English gardens and is only a short walk to a sandy Pacific Ocean beach. Summerland, adjacent to the Santa Barbara comunity of Montecito, is a charming seaside village with a variety of restaurants and shops.

Inn on Summer Hill
2529 Lillie Avenue
Summerland, CA 93067
805-969-9998
800-845-5566

Mimosa Truffles

Guests at the Inn on Summer Hill by the Sea sample these afternoon or evening treats while sipping champagne in their private whirlpools. A delicate orange and champagne flavor pervades these creamy truffles.

10 ounces bittersweet chocolate
2 egg yolks, beaten
1 cup powdered sugar, divided
½ cup heavy cream
4 tablespoons butter
4 tablespoons champagne
2 tablespoons orange-flavored liqueur

Also:
Cocoa
Paper or foil liners for miniature muffin cups

Melt bittersweet chocolate in a very heavy pan on low heat, stirring often until completely smooth.

In a separate bowl, cream egg yolks and ½ cup powdered sugar.

In a saucepan or double boiler, mix heavy cream, the other ½ cup powdered sugar, and butter, stirring constantly until the mixture boils.

Cool only slightly (you want to raise the temperature of the egg yolks to 160 degrees to kill salmonella bacteria). Gradually drizzle the hot mixture into the yolks while whisking constantly. Blend in the melted chocolate, champagne and liqueur.

Allow the mixture to cool in the refrigerator.

When set, roll into 1-inch diameter balls. Roll in cocoa and place in liners in small muffin cups.

Refrigerate until ready to serve.

Makes about 36 truffles

Substitutes for Chocolate

For unsweetened chocolate:
1 ounce (1 square) of unsweetened (bitter) chocolate equals 3 tablespoons cocoa powder plus 1 tablespoon shortening.

For semisweet chocolate:
1 ounce (1 square) of semisweet chocolate equals 1 ounce of unsweetened chocolate plus 1 tablespoon sugar.

For really good chocolate:
Are you kidding?

"The superiority of chocolate, both for health and nourishment, will soon give it the same preference over tea and coffee in America which it has in Spain."

—Thomas Jefferson, talking about hot chocolate as a drink (candy bars hadn't been invented yet), in a 1785 letter to John Adams

Rum Truffles

These serve as the best possible nightcap—one that's chocolate! This very adult candy (you can, indeed, taste the rum!) is pretty enough to give to fellow chocolate-lovers at the holidays.

½ cup heavy cream
3 tablespoons butter
3 cups semisweet chocolate chips
6 tablespoons favorite rum

Also:
⅔ cup white chocolate or vanilla chips or 6 ounce bar, frozen
Paper or foil liners for miniature muffin cups

Place cream and butter in a large glass bowl. Microwave until butter is melted. Add semisweet chips. Microwave on medium-high for 25 second intervals, stirring after each time, until chips are melted. (Cream and butter do not have to be thoroughly combined with chocolate.)

Pour the melted mixture into a food processor. Add the rum. Process for 5 minutes. Pour creamy mixture into an 8- or 9-inch pan lined with plastic wrap.

Cover loosely with plastic wrap (so condensation can escape) and place in the freezer. Freeze until about 1 hour before you are ready to roll the truffles into balls. Then remove from freezer and let sit.

Meanwhile, place the frozen white chocolate chips or pieces of white confection bar in a food processor. Process until the candy is ground to a powder (or grate the bar, which takes longer but is easier on the eardrums).

When truffle mixture is warm enough to scoop, roll a teaspoonful into a 1-inch ball, then roll in ground white chocolate. Repeat with the rest of the mixture.

Place truffles in a covered container in the freezer. Remove and place each in a lined muffin cup about 1 hour before serving.

Makes about 36 truffles

Country Garden Inn

This lovely old home, built in the 1850s as a coach house on the Silverado Trail, now welcomes guests indulging themselves in the Napa Valley's pleasures. Situated on 1.5 riverside acres, guests enjoy the rose garden, aviary and fountain, as well as their own unique guestroom. British Innkeeper Lisa Smith and her husband, George, are well known for their creative champagne breakfasts and tea-time treats.

Country Garden Inn
1815 Silverado Trail
Napa, CA 94558
707-255-1197
Fax 707-255-3112

Recipe Index

Entrees

Apricot Pancakes with Chocolate Orange Sauce, 12
Bittersweet Chocolate Souffles with White Chocolate and Rum Sauce, 14
Black Forest Stuffed French Toast, 16
Chocolate Banana Crepes in Apricot Sauce, 18
Chocolate Brownie Souffle, 20
Chocolate Chip Pancakes, 22
Chocolate Fondue, 23
Chocolate Chocolate Chip Waffles with Raspberry Syrup, 24
Chocolate Raspberry Blintzes, 26
Dark Chocolate Waffles, 28
Fudge Oven Souffle with Chocolate Sauce, 30
Overnight French Toast Puff, 32
White Chocolate Frittata with Raspberry Coulis, 34

Breads & Coffeecakes

Apple Fudge Cake, 36
Chocolate Bread Pudding, 37
Chocolate Icebox Rolls with Ginger Filling, 38
Chocolate Raspberry Date Bread, 40
Chocolate Zucchini Cake, 42
French Chocolate Coffeecake, 44
Mandarin Orange Chocolate Coffeecake, 46
MapleHedge Hungarian Coffeecake, 48
Mocha Supreme Coffeecake, 49
Toasted Walnut Fudge Bread, 50

Muffins, Scones & Popovers

Banana Chip Scones, 52
Banana Chocolate Chip Muffins, 53
Black Bottom Muffins, 54
Buttermilk Orange Scones, 56
Chocolate Chip Orange Scones, 57
Chocolate Lover's Muffins, 58
Chocolate Macadamia Muffins, 60
Chocolate Popovers, 62
Double Chocolate Almond Muffins, 63
Double Chocolate Banana Muffins, 64
Espresso Chip Muffins, 65
Double Chocolate Cherry Muffins, 66
Double Chocolate Delight Muffins, 68
Low-Cholesterol Double Chocolate Muffins, 70
Lower-Fat Banana Chunk Muffins, 72
Magnificent Miniature Muffins, 73
Mocha Chocolate Chip Scones, 74
Mocha Walnut Chip Muffins, 76
Raspberry Chocolate Chip Muffins, 78
Spicy Chocolate Pumpkin Muffins, 79
Spicy Mocha Apple Muffins, 80

Desserts for Breakfast, Tea-Time & Snacks

Chocolate Apricot Torte, 82
Chocolate Cherry Bon-Bon Crepes, 84
Chocolate Heaven Logs, 86
Chocolate-Glazed Shortbread "Doggie Bones," 88
Chocolate Rum Pound Cake with Fudge Glaze, 90
Christmas Brownie Alaska, 92
Cook's Double Chocolate Rebels, 94
Cowboy Cookies, 95
Deep Dark Chocolate Fudge Cake, 96
Easy Frozen Chocolate Mousse Cups, 98
Espresso Brownies, 99
Flourless Chocolate Torte, 100
Fudge Mound Cookies, 102
Grandma Lulu's Chocolate Pound Cake, 104
Heavenly Montana-Sized Chocolate Chip Cookies, 105
Hint of Mint Chocolate Torte, 106
Old-Fashioned Chocolate Chip Oatmeal Cookies, 108
Red Devil Mocha Cake, 110
Toffee Bars, 111
Chocolate Truffles, 112
Kahlua Tea-Time Truffles, 114
Mimosa Truffles, 116
Rum Truffles, 118